BUSINESS ISSUES, COMPETITION AND ENTREPRENEURSHIP

YOUNG WORKERS IN THE SHADOW OF THE GREAT RECESSION

ANALYSIS AND PERSPECTIVES

BUSINESS ISSUES, COMPETITION AND ENTREPRENEURSHIP

Additional books in this series can be found on Nova's website under the Series tab.

Additional e-books in this series can be found on Nova's website under the e-book tab.

BUSINESS ISSUES, COMPETITION AND ENTREPRENEURSHIP

YOUNG WORKERS IN THE SHADOW OF THE GREAT RECESSION

ANALYSIS AND PERSPECTIVES

NICHOLE CALDWELL
EDITOR

nova publishers
New York

Library of Congress Cataloging-in-Publication Data

ISBN: 978-1-63482-184-1

Published by Nova Science Publishers, Inc. † New York

CONTENTS

PREFACE

Young adults in the United States have experienced higher rates of unemployment and lower rates of labor force participation than the general population for at least two decades. The Great Recession exacerbated this phenomenon. Despite a substantial labor market recovery from 2009 through 2014, vulnerable populations—including the nation's young adults—continue to experience higher rates of unemployment. Meanwhile, changes in labor market conditions, including globalization and automation, have reduced the availability of well-paid, secure jobs for less-educated persons, particularly those jobs that provide opportunity for advancement. Furthermore, data suggest that young workers entering the labor market are affected by a long-running increase in the use of "contingent" work arrangements, characterized by contracted, part-time, temporary, and seasonal work. This book summarizes insights from the Survey of Young Workers and related research in the field; and it frames policy and research issues for future consideration by the Federal Reserve Board and others interested in young workers.

Chapter 1 – This report presents the findings of a survey conducted in December 2013 that explores the experiences and expectations of young Americans entering the labor market.

Chapter 2 – Congress has indicated a strong interest in ensuring that today's young people—those ages 16 through 24—attain the education and employment experience necessary to make the transition to adulthood as skilled workers and taxpayers. In the wake of the December 2007-June 2009 recession, questions remain about the employment prospects of youth today and the possible effects on their future earnings and participation in the labor market.

- Over the past decade, teens and young adults have experienced a precipitous decline in employment and a corresponding increase in unemployment. In 2000, their employment to population (E/P) ratio was about 60%. Their E/P ratio steadily eroded even when the economy grew in the mid-2000s. The December 2007-June 2009 recession resulted in record low employment (based on the E/P ratio) for this population. Since the official end of the recession, younger workers have continued to fare poorly in the labor market. In 2012, youth ages 16 through 24 had an E/P ratio of 46.0% and a rate of unemployment at 16.2%. This is compared to an E/P ratio of 75.7% and an unemployment rate of 7.0% for workers of prime working age, 25 through 54.
- Recent declining E/P ratios for young people are likely due to decreasing demand for labor generally and youth foregoing work for higher education. Youth may decide to pursue education because of dismal employment prospects and the growing need for more education to be successful in the labor market.
- Throughout the post-World War II period, the E/P ratio has been highest for white youth, followed by Hispanic youth. Black and Asian youth have been the least likely to be employed. For black youth, this is likely due to lower educational attainment. Lower rates of employment for Asian youth are likely attributable to their increasing participation in postsecondary education. Young black males in particular have had the lowest E/P ratios.
- Beginning in the 1970s, the E/P ratios for women increased as they entered the workforce in greater numbers. The gender difference in the E/P ratio for teens and young adults began to narrow in the 1990s, likely due to greater high school and college attainment among females and other factors.
- Lower E/P ratios—and simultaneous increases in unemployment—for young people appear to be due to a confluence of factors. Youth have less education and experience relative to older workers. In general, firms are more likely to hire workers with more experience and availability, which puts young workers at a disadvantage. Young workers may especially face challenges in landing a job during tough economic times.

The consequences of decreasing E/P ratios and increasing unemployment among youth have not been fully explored. Preliminary research in this area has hypothesized that reductions in human capital, such as deterioration of skills and foregone work experience, may have lasting impacts on employability and wages of youth. Some studies show that on average, early youth unemployment has negative effects on incomes but not as strong effects on future unemployment; however, youth entering the labor market during severe downturns in the economy appear to have relatively lower wages in the longer term.

In: Young Workers in the Shadow ...
Editor: Nichole Caldwell
ISBN: 978-1-63482-184-1

Chapter 1

IN THE SHADOW OF THE GREAT RECESSION: EXPERIENCES AND PERSPECTIVES OF YOUNG WORKERS*

Alexandra Brown, Nuha Elmaghrabi, Lindsey Holthaus and Heidi Kaplan

EXECUTIVE SUMMARY

Young adults in the United States have experienced higher rates of unemployment and lower rates of labor force participation than the general population for at least two decades.[1] The Great Recession exacerbated this phenomenon.[2] Despite a substantial labor market recovery from 2009 through 2014, vulnerable populations—including the nation's young adults—continue to experience higher rates of unemployment.[3]

Meanwhile, changes in labor market conditions, including globalization and automation, have reduced the availability of well-paid, secure jobs for less-educated persons, particularly those jobs that provide opportunity for advancement. Furthermore, data suggest that young workers entering the labor market are affected by a long-running increase in the use of "contingent" work

---

* This is an edited, reformatted and augmented version of a report issued by the Board of Governors of the Federal Reserve, November 2014. The Federal Reserve Board's Division of Consumer and Community Affairs (DCCA) conducted the Survey of Young Workers for this report.

arrangements, characterized by contracted, part-time, temporary, and seasonal work.[4]

In light of these trends, in 2013, the Federal Reserve Board's Division of Consumer and Community Affairs began exploring the experiences and expectations of young Americans entering the labor market. Staff reviewed existing research and engaged external research and policy experts to identify the potential economic implications of these labor market trends on young workers.

This initial exploration raised several questions about the experiences of young workers that were not fully explained by existing data. In response, the Federal Reserve conducted a survey, the Survey of Young Workers, in December 2013 to develop a deeper understanding of the forces at play. The online survey was intended to be exploratory—ultimately confirming some insights and highlighting areas worthy of additional study. The Survey of Young Workers was administered by GfK (formerly Knowledge Networks), using its Internet panel.[5] The 2,097 survey respondents ranged in age from 18 to 30. Details about the survey, its methodology, and limitations can be found in the body of the report and in a methodological appendix (Appendix A: Methodology).

This report is intended to serve two principal purposes. First, it summarizes insights from the Survey of Young Workers and related research in the field. Second, it frames policy and research issues for future consideration by the Federal Reserve Board and others interested in young workers.

Key Findings

This report presents findings from the December 2013 survey. Key findings include the following:

Connecting Education and the Labor Market

Educational programs and goals should align with labor market demands in order to prepare students to join the workforce

- Students need information on potential job outcomes from a variety of educational options to guide their career-planning decisions. In fact, respondents noted that uncertainty about job outcomes is a barrier to enrollment in postsecondary education.

- The current gap in alignment between education and the labor market may contribute to the number of young workers who have not found paid work in their chosen field of study. Only 42 percent of working respondents in the survey have a job that is closely related to their field of study.
- Many high school students are not receiving adequate information about job planning. In the survey, 63 percent of respondents reported that they received information about jobs and careers during high school, while 24 percent of respondents reported that they received none.
- This situation is similar for college students. Among respondents who attended any college, 66 percent received information about jobs during these years, while 22 percent reported that they received none.
- According to survey respondents, school counselors and teachers are the primary source of job information in both high school and college. Hence, educational institutions have an opportunity to provide students with more information about the labor market.

Young workers are responding to the labor market's increasing demandfor postsecondary credentials and degrees

- Thirty-seven percent of the respondents reported that they have the level of education and training needed for the type of job that they would like to hold in the next five years. As expected, the respondents' confidence in their education increases with each level of attainment.
- In response to the need for more education, nearly one-third of the total respondents are currently enrolled in an education or training program.

The labor market rewards education and work experience with career paths and higher earnings

- Respondents with higher levels of education are more likely to be employed, to be working in a field related to their education and training, and to characterize themselves as being in a "career" rather than "just a job."

- Respondents with higher levels of education and work experience are more likely to have higher earnings and to be able to cover their monthly household expenses.
- Respondents with early work experience, such as a high school job, are more likely to be currently working and more likely to have a full-time job than those who did not work during high school.
- Workers with a postsecondary degree have the most opportunity for upward mobility, with 39 percent describing their job as a "career" and 23 percent reporting they have "just a job."[6]

The ability to pay for postsecondary education affects a young adult's decision to enroll

- Nonstudents who are interested in additional education named financial considerations—including not being able to afford school or not wanting to take out loans—as their top barriers to enrollment.
- Twenty-three percent of respondents reported that the financial benefits of their education do not outweigh the cost of their education.[7] These respondents are more likely to have student loans associated with their education.
- Meanwhile, respondents who reported a high financial value for the cost of their education are more likely to have received a scholarship, cash for their education, or financial assistance from an employer for their education. One possible explanation for this finding is that because these respondents are less likely to have student debt, their perceived return on investment is typically higher than their counterparts with student loans.

Job Fit

Job satisfaction is driven by compensation and schedule

- According to the survey, 66 percent of respondents are somewhat satisfied or very satisfied with their job arrangements over the past five years. The satisfaction of these respondents is attributed to their compensation and their schedule.

- Likewise, lack of job satisfaction is driven by compensation and schedule.

Despite the importance of education and work experience, intangibles still play a role in the labor market

- According to the survey, landing a job is still heavily based on personal connections. Respondents identified personal networks as a primary source in their job search process.
- Demographics also play an important role in labor market outcomes. For example, non-Hispanic white respondents are more likely than other racial and ethnic groups to have early job information and experience. This subgroup was more likely to receive this information from their parents, friends and family, and their place of work. This group is also more likely to have held a job while in high school and college.

Upward Mobility

"Traditional jobs" (defined as permanent, full-time jobs) are associated with "careers" and upward mobility, while the opportunities associated with contingent work are less clear

- Respondents with traditional jobs are more likely to have higher salaries and wages than those with temporary or part-time employment.
- Full-time workers are more likely to have received a promotion in the past year and to perceive opportunities for advancement in their job than part-time workers.

The lack of labor market opportunities may have pushed workers to accept jobs for which they are overqualified

- Twenty-eight percent of working respondents reported that they are overqualified for their current job. Respondents with an associate's or bachelor's degree are most likely to report they are overqualified for their job.
- Less than one-third of those who described themselves as overqualified for their current job are working in a field related to their education or training.
- The data suggest that in some cases less-educated workers have been pushed out of previously available, well-paid, secure jobs that are filled by overqualified workers. And, as a result, 83 percent of those seeking a job have not completed a postsecondary degree.

Young Workers' Unemployment

Close to half of respondents who do not have a paid job are seeking paid employment

- Most of the unemployed respondents have low levels of educational attainment, including 83 percent who have not completed a postsecondary degree.
- Only 20 percent of the job seekers had a job interview in the four weeks prior to completing the Survey of Young Workers.

Young Workers' Outlook

Young workers value job stability

- When given the choice, young workers generally prefer steady employment (67 percent) to higher pay (30 percent).
- Going forward, young workers expect greater job stability than they have experienced to date. Young workers generally have not experienced much job stability, as 29 percent have held a single, full-time job for one year, and another 14 percent have held a single, full-time job for five years. However, they expect greater job stability in the future, with 43 percent expecting to have a single, full-time job for the next five years.

Education, work experience, andjob opportunities are the main drivers of a young worker's outlook about their job future

- In the survey, 45 percent of respondents reported that they are optimistic about their job future. Respondents with higher levels of education, work experience, and job opportunities are more likely to be optimistic about their job future than respondents who lack such skills and experiences.
- Likewise, the 21 percent of respondents who reported that they are pessimistic about their job future are more likely to lack economic opportunity, job experience, and education.
- In the survey, 34 percent of respondents are not sure about their job future.

Policy and Research Implications

The survey demonstrates the association between postsecondary education and positive labor market outcomes, ranging from optimism about one's job future to higher earnings. Hence, it is critical that young workers receive appropriate information that enables them to select an educational program that maximizes their job opportunities. Young adults considering postsecondary education must choose from a range of public, nonprofit, and for-profit institutions offering an assortment of degrees and training programs. However, limited information is available to young workers regarding the likelihood of landing a job or the expected salary from these alternative options. The decision is further complicated for the majority of potential students who do not have the personal resources to pay for their education upfront or lack the ability to earn a full scholarship.

Because education plays such an important role in a young person's career opportunities, additional research on the outcomes from various educational paths is essential. School teachers, counselors, and other providers of career information also need these valuable resources to properly advise individuals as they develop a career path.

The Survey of Young Workers is intended to provide a general overview of individuals at the onset of their workforce experience. The report highlights some notable differences based on respondent characteristics such as race and ethnicity, gender, and geographic location. These preliminary findings and the policy solutions that seek to address them merit additional analysis. While the survey adds to the body of knowledge provided by previous surveys and research on this topic, much remains to be explored. The Federal Reserve intends for this report to help shape future inquiry among workforce researchers, policy-makers, and practitioners. To this end, the Federal Reserve will make the survey's data available to the public. In addition, the Federal Reserve will encourage additional use of these data for research both within the Federal Reserve System and among external parties.

INTRODUCTION

In recent years, the labor market has made a substantial recovery from the Great Recession. For example, the U.S. unemployment rate decreased from 10 percent in October 2009 to 5.9 percent by September 2014.[8] Yet despite this overall improvement, vulnerable populations—including the nation's young adults—continue to experience higher rates of unemployment compared with the national average. In September 2014, unemployment among those ages 16 to 24 remained just over two times (2.3) that of the national average.[9] In 2014, unemployment gradually improved among 18- to 24-year-olds and unemployment among workers from ages 25 to 34 tracked the national average.[10] According to the Economic Policy Institute, young workers have historically experienced disproportionate increases in unemployment during economic downturns.[11]

While a recent decline in unemployment is encouraging, the accompanying decrease in labor force participation among young people is a cause for concern. The labor force participation rate for 16- to-24-yearolds has declined from about 66 percent in 2000 to roughly 55 percent in mid-2014. In fact, the decline in participation for this group has been so large that it accounts for roughly 40 percent of the downtrend in aggregate participation over this 15-year period. While this trend has been documented by a number of researchers, a cohesive explanation has remained elusive.[12]

In addition to higher rates of unemployment since the recession, workers face broader changes to the labor markets. Globalization, automation, and improved efficiencies in the workplace are changing how employment and training programs connect workers to jobs, particularly those that require special skills and provide for wage advancement. As employers seek new ways to make the employment relationship more flexible, they have increasingly relied on a variety of arrangements popularly known as "contingent work." The use of independent contractors and part-time, temporary, seasonal, and leased workers has expanded in recent years.[13]

In December 2013, the Federal Reserve Board's Division of Consumer and Community Affairs conducted the Survey of Young Workers. The survey is an initial inquiry into the work experiences and expectations of young workers. In this report, the term "young workers" is used to refer to the full sample of respondents as workers and potential workers. The Federal Reserve conducted the survey using an Internet panel. The survey focuses on young workers' outlook on the labor market, connections between education and labor market outcomes, job fit and upward mobility, unemployment, labor market expectations, and self-employment. Some findings confirm other research results, others provide new insights, and still others raise questions that suggest areas for further investigation. Other literature and research also are used to supplement the findings from the survey.

About the Survey

The Survey of Young Workers was administered by GfK, an online consumer research company, on behalf of the Federal Reserve. The survey was conducted using a sample of adults between the ages 18 to 30 from the KnowledgePanel, a proprietary, probability-based web panel of more than 50,000 individuals from randomly sampled households; the sample was designed to be representative of the U.S. population.

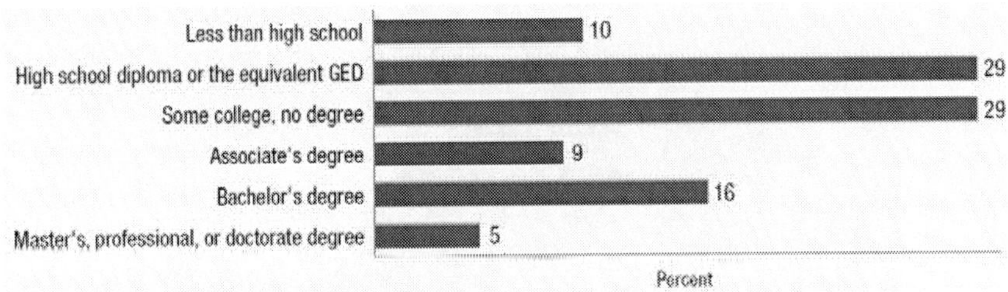

Note: Number of responses is 2,097.

Figure 1. Distribution of educational attainment; Percent of survey respondents with indicated level of education completed.

The data collection for the Survey of Young Workers began on December 4, 2013, and concluded on December 17, 2013. E-mails were sent to 4,242 randomly selected respondents from the KnowledgePanel. The 2,097 respondents represented 49 percent of those contacted. The median time to complete the survey was approximately 14 minutes.

This report summarizes key findings from the Survey of Young Workers. The numbers cited in this report are derived from the survey unless otherwise noted. All data are weighted to yield estimates for the U.S. population.

Profile of Respondents

The Survey of Young Workers respondents were asked to describe three distinct aspects of their employment path and to treat each aspect of their work path independently: (1) education and training, (2) experience as a paid employee, and (3) self-employment activities.

The survey sample is weighted to reflect the educational attainment of 18- to 30-year-olds nationwide. As such, 10 percent of the respondents have less than a high school education, 29 percent have completed high school, 29 percent have some college experience, 9 percent hold an associate's degree, and 21 percent hold a bachelor's degree or higher (figure 1). Thirty-two percent of respondents are currently enrolled as students in either an educational or training program. Of those enrolled, 73 percent are full-time students and 26 percent are part-time students.

In the survey, 23 percent of the respondents are enrolled as full-time students and 9 percent are enrolled as part-time students (figure 2). Of the total sample, 68 percent of respondents are not currently enrolled in an education or training program.

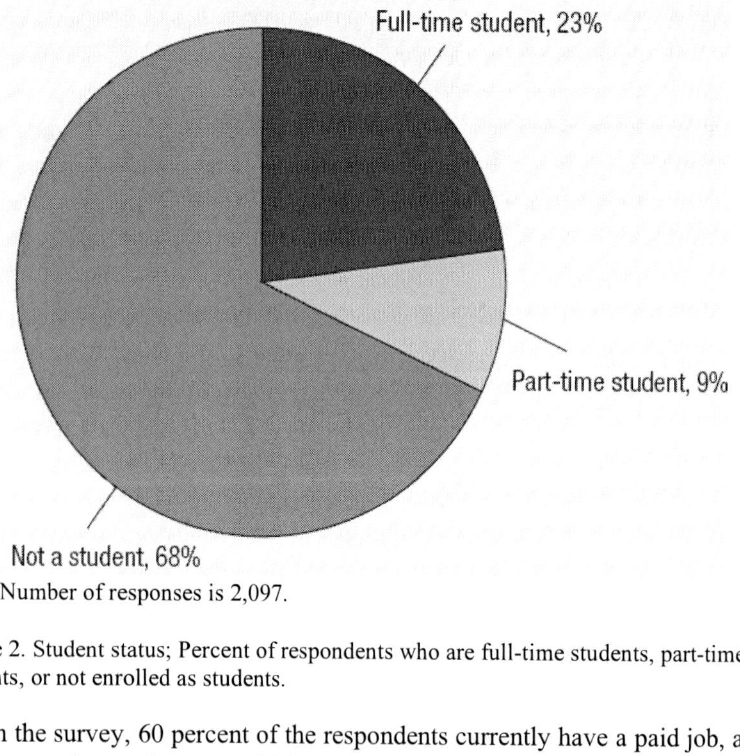

Note: Number of responses is 2,097.

Figure 2. Student status; Percent of respondents who are full-time students, part-time students, or not enrolled as students.

In the survey, 60 percent of the respondents currently have a paid job, and 40 percent do not have a paid job (figure 3). Of those with a paid job, 67 percent work full time, and 33 percent work part time. For respondents who do not have a paid job, nearly half (47 percent) are unemployed and actively seeking employment, while slightly more than half (53 percent) are not seeking a paid job. Sixteen percent of the respondents are engaged in some form of self-employment. More specifically, 4 percent of respondents own a business, 2 percent run a nonprofit organization, and 10 percent generate income from activities where they are their "own boss."

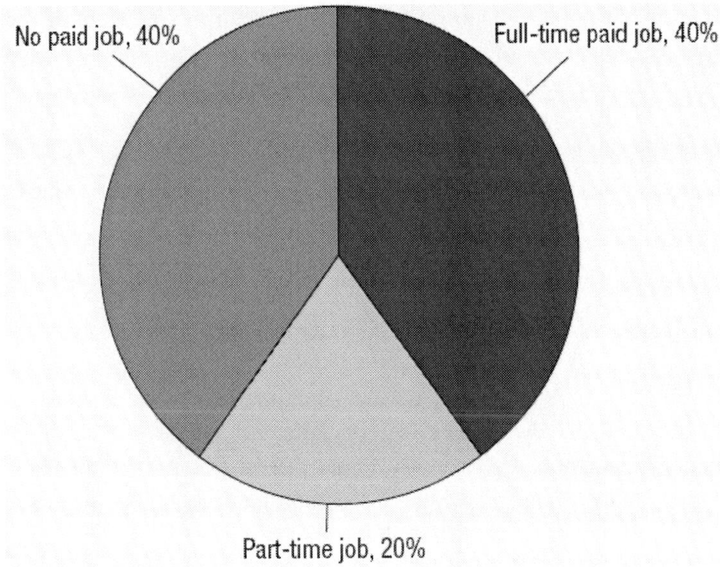

Note: Number of responses is 2,097.

Figure 3. Paid work status; Percent of respondents who are working full time,working part time, or not working a paid job.

Connecting Education and the Labor Market

The 21st century workforce is shaping up to look quite different from the workforce of the 20th century. The U.S job market has seen a steady decline in well-paid, secure jobs, such as in manufacturing, and an increase in demand for cognitive knowledge, skills, and abilities. This change in the job market has meant a shift from jobs that require no more than a high school diploma to jobs that require at least some postsecondary education. As evidence of this shift, in the aftermath of the recession, college-educated workers continue to fare significantly better than those without a postsecondary degree.[14]

Connecting education and the labor market is increasingly important for young workers. With the labor market's growing demand for formal educational attainment, choosing a postsecondary program is the first substantial investment decision many young people will make. Young adults need to understand the risks and rewards associated with their choice of postsecondary institution and field of study. As the cost of certificates and degrees grows and the labor market demands shift, prospective students need more information to guide their choices and to ensure higher returns on their investment. Furthermore, aligning education more closely with careers promotes student success, as people with a sense of where they are going are more likely to achieve their desired goal.[15]

As described further below, the survey responses supported the notion that postsecondary degrees are associated with greater optimism about the labor market, early career planning, and higher earnings.

Rising Demand for Educational Attainment

Given the changing nature of the labor market, many workers are not confident that their current level of education is suitable for the job market. For example, in 2011, a Pew study found that just under half of the general population believes they have the necessary training to be successful in a career.[16] In the same study, high school graduates were less clear about what they needed but mainly agreed on the importance continued education at some level.[17]

In the Survey of Young Workers, 37 percent of the respondents believe they have the level of education and training needed for the type of job that they would like to hold in the next five years. As expected, the respondents' confidence in their education increases with each level of attainment, with 32 percent of those with a high school diploma, 42 percent with an associate's degree, 60 percent of those with a bachelor's degree, and 73 percent of those with a master's, professional, or doctorate degree reporting that they have the necessary level of education. (For a discussion of confidence and gender, see box 1.)

Respondents to the survey are continuing to increase their level of education and training in response to labor market demand. Nearly one-third (32 percent) of the total respondents are enrolled in an education or training program. The student respondents include 42 percent of those who reported they lack the necessary level of education. Notably, of those who reported they do have the necessary level of education for their desired job in the next five years, 26 percent are students.

Box 1. Compared to Young Men, Young Women Lack Confidence in Their Educational Attainment

In the Survey of Young Workers, as in national data, more female respondents are enrolled in education or training programs than men. Likewise, more women have incurred debt for education than men. Yet, female respondents are less likely to be confident that they have the level of education needed for the next five years in the workforce. In fact, when the level of education is controlled for, male respondents are more confident in their level of training than women.

Nearly three-fourths (73 percent) of the student respondents are enrolled full time, while one-fourth are enrolled part time. Most of the students are enrolled in a degree program, including 20 percent working toward an associate's degree, 44 percent working toward a bachelor's degree, and 14 percent working toward a graduate or professional degree.

According to a study by Georgetown University, certificates are the fastest-growing postsecondary credential awarded over the past several decades, as they are relatively cheap, can be completed quickly, and may lead to industry-based certifications. Georgetown University reports that certificates have grown from 6 percent of postsecondary awards in 1980 to 22 percent in 2012.[18]

In the Survey of Young Workers, 7 percent of respondents are enrolled in a vocational program. Although the survey does not measure total certificates earned, it appears that this group is underrepresented in the sample.

Alignment of Education and Career Path

In order for students to get the most out of their education, it is important that educational programs and goals align with the needs of the labor market. This alignment is key, as workers attempting to satisfy the labor market's increasing demand for education must also identify a field of study that that will offer career opportunities. For individual workers, the connection between education and the labor market should occur during their educational process.

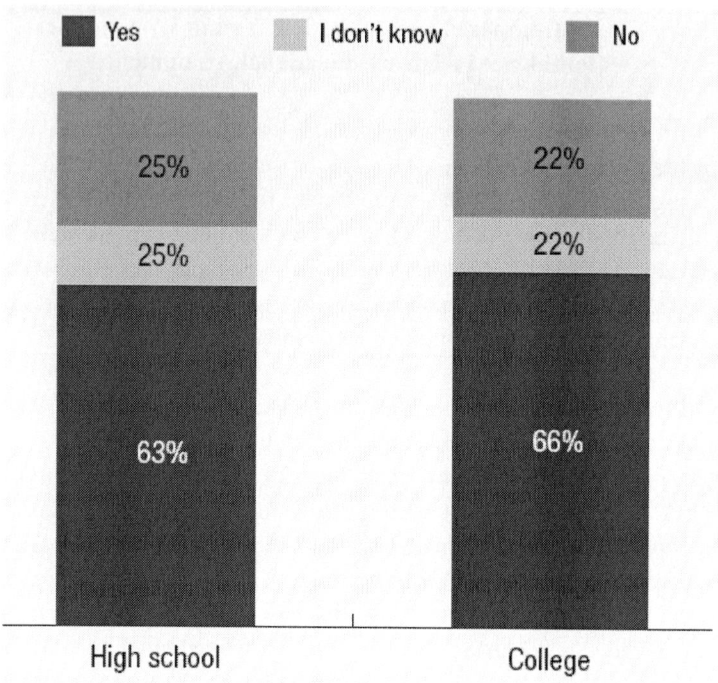

Figure 4. Many students did receive information about jobs and careers in school; Received information about jobs and careers in....

In the Survey of Young Workers, 63 percent of respondents reported that they received information about jobs and careers during high school (figure 4). Although the survey does not measure the value or accuracy of this information, nearly two-thirds of students are obtaining labor market information during their high school years. High school staff is a key source of job information, as three-fourths of those who received this information credited their high school counselors and teachers as the source (figure 5). While in high school, respondents who received information about jobs also noted personal networks, including parents (57 percent) and friends and family (48 percent) as the source.

Some high school students (21 percent) reported that the information they received helped them find a job. Without knowing whether the high school students are seeking a job, it is difficult to assess the implications of this number.

That said, 25 percent of respondents reported that they did not receive any information about jobs during high school. An additional 11 percent are not sure if they received such information or not. This represents a substantial number of respondents who exited the K–12 educational system without formal or informal communication about planning for a job or career.

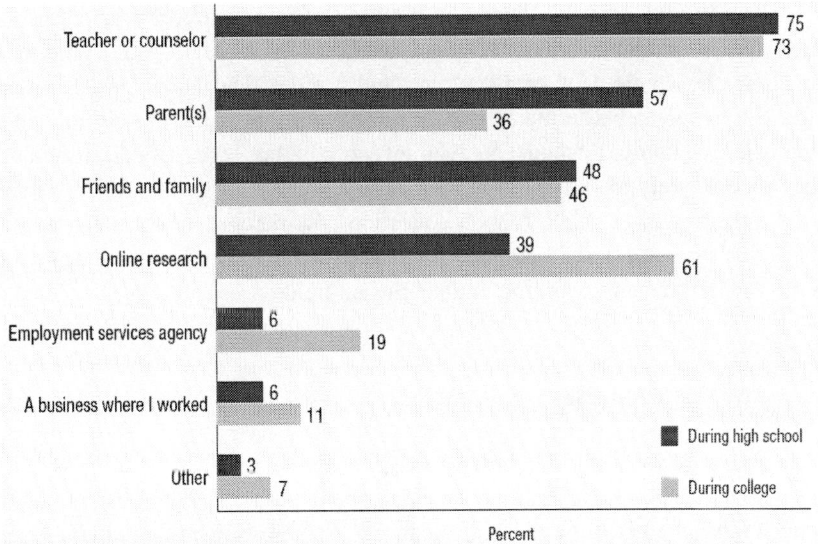

Note: Number of responses for "during high school" is 2,097; for "during college" is 1,548.

Figure 5. Teachers and counselors are the largest source of job and career information; Sources of information about careers and jobs (respondents may select more than one response).

The Survey of Young Workers found that college students received job and career information at similar rates as high school students. Among respondents who attended any college, 66 percent received information about jobs during these years. Likewise, for those who received information, 73 percent reported receiving this information from school counselors and teachers. College students are more likely to rely on online resources when seeking job information (61 percent).

Again, similar to the high school students, 22 percent of those who attended college reported that they did not receive information about jobs and careers at this time. An additional 10 percent were not sure. Per the previous comment, this represents a sizable number of respondents who participated in postsecondary education without receiving formal or informal information about jobs and careers.

College students offer a striking difference from high school students when considering whether the information they received helped them obtain a job. Forty percent of the respondents who received information from their college reported that the information helped them find a job.

The current gaps in alignment between education and the labor market may contribute to the number of young workers who have not found paid work in their chosen field of study. Accordingly, more than half (51 percent) of working respondents in the survey do not have a job that is closely related to their field of study. Respondents who invest in higher levels of education have been more likely to find a job in their field of study. To that point, 26 percent of workers with a high school education, 67 percent of workers with a bachelor's degree, and 84 percent of workers with a master's degree or greater reported that they are working in their chosen field.

Cost of Postsecondary Education

The ability to pay for postsecondary education affects a young adult's decision to enroll in a training or educational program. The cost of higher education has grown more rapidly than median family income, leaving many students and families with little choice but to borrow money.[19] Moreover, the average debt is substantial, which could also limit career choices, as students may need to take jobs that allow them to pay off their loans.

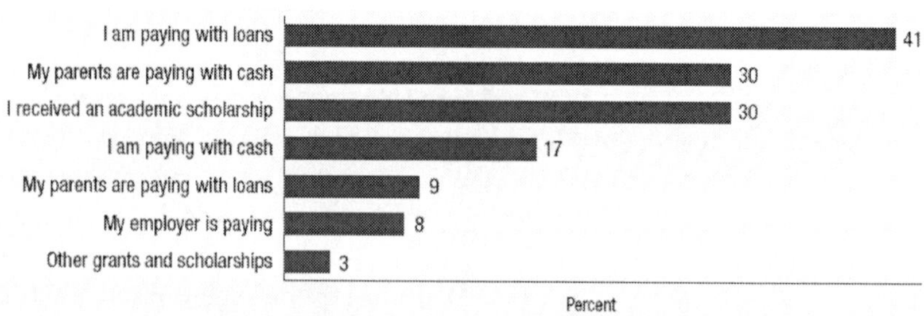

Note: Number of responses is 648.

Figure 6. Loans are the most frequent source of financing for postsecondary education; Financing used to pay for current enrollment (respondents may select more than one response).

In the Survey of Young Workers, students reported that they are financing their education with cash, loans, and scholarships (figure 6). At 41 percent, personal loans are the form of financing most commonly used by students who are currently enrolled in school, while 9 percent of student respondents have parents that took out loans for their education. Thirty percent of student respondents have parents that are paying for their education with cash, and 17 percent are paying with their own cash. Thirty percent of students have academic scholarships. And, finally, 8 percent of respondents have employers paying for their education.

Students may use more than one source of financing to pay for their postsecondary education. A survey by the Heldrich Center for Workforce Development found that 65 percent of recent college graduates relied on two sources of financing, namely government loans (56 percent) and family savings (49 percent).[20]

Financial barriers top the list of reasons that nonstudents who are interested in additional education do not enroll. Half of the nonstudents in the survey are interested in additional education. However, 63 percent of nonstudents who are interested in additional education do not want to borrow money and 58 percent reported that they are not able to afford an educational program.

The value of additional education in the current job market is also important for these respondents. Forty-four percent of respondents interested in additional education reported being concerned about not being able to land a job after completing the program and 39 percent reported that they do not know which program would improve their job opportunities. These challenges to enrollment again speak to the importance of reliable information about postsecondary education outcomes.

Valuing Postsecondary Education

Survey respondents were asked whether they believe the lifetime financial benefits of their most recent educational program outweigh the program's financial cost.[21] In the survey, 41 percent of respondents reported that their educational investment is greater than the cost of their education ("high valuers") (figure 7). Meanwhile, 23 percent reported that the financial value of their education is smaller than the cost of the education ("low valuers").

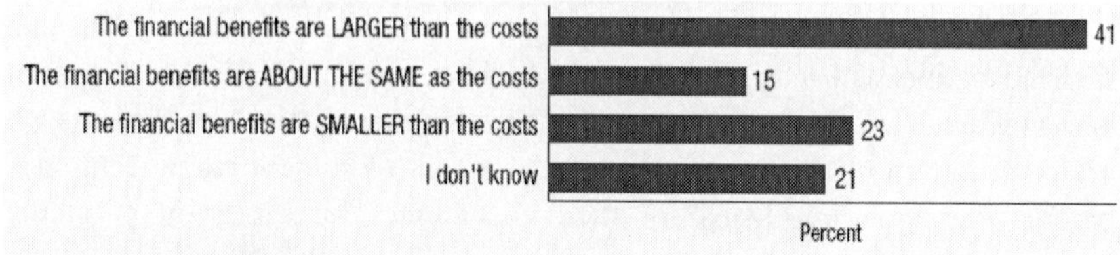

Note: Number of responses is 1,209.

Figure 7. Less than half report that the financial benefits of postsecondary education are larger than the costs; Perceived value of postsecondary education.

High valuers are more likely to have an educational experience that aligns with both their current job and their employment aspirations. They are more likely to be working in a career that is closely related to their field of study (72 percent) than low valuers (39 percent). In addition, high valuers tend to be more confident that their education is sufficient for the type of job they would like to hold in the next five years (58 percent) than low valuers (39 percent).

High valuers are also more likely to have employment with more stability and opportunities for upward mobility. For example, these respondents are more likely to have full-time employment (77 percent) than low valuers (71 percent). High valuers are more likely to be in a "career" (46 percent) with a salary (48 percent) than low valuers (24 percent and 25 percent, respectively). Finally, high valuers are more likely to believe there is opportunity for advancement at their current job (66 percent) than low valuers (44 percent).

In the survey, respondents who are currently enrolled in an educational or training program were asked how they are financing this undertaking. High valuers are more likely to be paying for their education with upfront cash and scholarships, while low valuers are more likely to have loans to be paid after they enter the workforce. High valuers are more likely to be paying for their education with their own cash (26 percent) or cash from their parents (26 percent) than low valuers (12 percent and 13 percent, respectively). High valuers are also more likely to have a scholarship (32 percent) or an employer to cover tuition (20 percent) than low valuers (22 percent and 15 percent, respectively). One possible explanation for this finding is that because these respondents are less likely to have student debt, their perceived return on investment is high.

Meanwhile, low valuers are more likely to be paying for their education with personal loans (68 percent) than high valuers (42 percent). Because these respondents took on student debt, they may have to earn more to feel that they received an appropriate return on their investment.

Importance of Early Work Experience

National data show that 66 percent of all students balance a full- or part-time job while attending school, including work–study.[22] According to the Bureau of Labor Statistics (BLS), 20 percent of high school students are employed and 50 percent of college students ages 16 to 24 are employed while attending school.[23] Although some students work to meet their financial needs, students also maintain jobs to gain early work experience before embarking on a longer-range career. In the Survey of Young Workers, 57 percent of all full-time students and 55 percent of all part-time students are working and attending school. (For a discussion on racial and ethnic early work experience, see box 2.)

Box 2. Non-Hispanic White Respondents Have More Early Work Experience

In the Survey of Young Workers, non-Hispanic white respondents are more likely to have worked in high school and college than respondents of other racial and ethnic groups. Moreover, non-Hispanic white respondents are more likely to have received information about jobs during high school and are more likely to have held a paid job at this time. This group primarily received this information from their parents, friends and family, and their place of work.

In a 2014 study by the Brookings Institution, teen employment is associated with improved employment and earnings' outcomes later in life. Although problems finding work affected all young people in the past decade, those with work experience, those with higher levels of education, and those from higher income households have been more successful in the labor market. Therefore, for teens and young adults, employment history is a strong predictor of current employment. Because teen and young adult unemployment is concentrated among less-educated and low-income individuals, this phenomenon threatens the upward mobility of already vulnerable populations.[24]

Consistent with the Brookings findings, respondents to the Survey of Young Workers who had a paid job during high school are more likely to be currently working (69 percent) than those who did not have a paid job during high school (48 percent). Furthermore, respondents who worked during high school are more likely to have a full-time job (70 percent) than those who did not work during high school (60 percent). Some of this relationship may be explained by those who did not work while in high school being more focused on preparing for college. Nevertheless, even among persons who went to college, the survey indicates that those who complemented their study with work experience had better job outcomes.

The Survey of Young Workers indicates that high school and college students who complemented their study with work experience had better job outcomes. For example, respondents who gained work experience during school are more likely to be working in a job related to their educational field (49 percent) than those who did not work during school (31 percent). Likewise, respondents who combined work experience and education are more likely to be working in a job they perceive as a career (29 percent) or a stepping stone to a career (39 percent) than those who did not (19 percent and 29 percent, respectively).

The Survey of Young Workers suggests that the Great Recession affected the percentage of high school students in the workforce. Post-recession graduates, those age 18 to 21 years old, are less likely to have worked in high school (39 percent) than respondents graduating during the recession, ages 22 to 25 years old (57 percent) or pre-recession, ages 26 to 30 percent (62 percent).

JOB FIT

The existing literature suggests a vast majority of young workers appear satisfied in their jobs. However, many young workers have made concessions in the near term, as they forgo traditional work or higher pay in favor of a steady job. A survey by Pew Research Center from early 2012 found that half (49 percent) of young Americans ages 18 to 34 said that they took a job they did not want so that they could pay their bills.[25]

Job Satisfaction

According to the Survey of Young Workers, 66 percent of respondents are somewhat satisfied or very satisfied with their job arrangements over the past five years (figure 8). The satisfaction of these respondents is attributed to their compensation and their schedule (figure 9). For example, one respondent stated, “my jobs had decent hours, decent pay, and I was never involuntarily unemployed." Another stated, "I got experience that I can utilize in other fields/jobs, and the payment I received helped me get through that certain [sic] time."

Thirty-three percent of respondents who have held a job in the past five years reported being dissatisfied with their job arrangements. Again, pay and schedule are the leading reasons for this level of dissatisfaction (figure 10). One respondent said, "Employers didn't pay well enough to survive without taking on another job."

Job Attainment

A 2012 study by the Heldrich Center found that job seekers turned to two primary sources to obtain their first jobs. About 60 percent turned to personal connections to help find employment. And the same number turned to the Internet to search formal online job sources, such as Monster or Career-Builder, or employers' job-site boards. The Heldrich Center found there was much less reliance on college placement offices (less than one in three) and employment agencies or government job centers (16 percent).[26]

In the Survey of Young Workers, respondents also identify personal connections as a primary source in a job candidate's search process. In the survey, 14 percent of working respondents had a parent who provided the contact information for their current job, and 26 percent of respondents said that networks of friends and other family played a role in finding their current job.

Likewise, in the Survey of Young Workers, employment services do not play a key role in finding a job for the respondents. Despite respondents reporting that teachers and school counselors are a key source of information while in high school and college, only 10 percent of respondents credited school counselors with helping them obtain their current job. Furthermore, young workers do not use employment centers with any great regularity, as 9 percent of respondents with college experience used employment centers in their pursuit of employment and only 8 percent of working respondents credit job centers as the source for landing their current job.

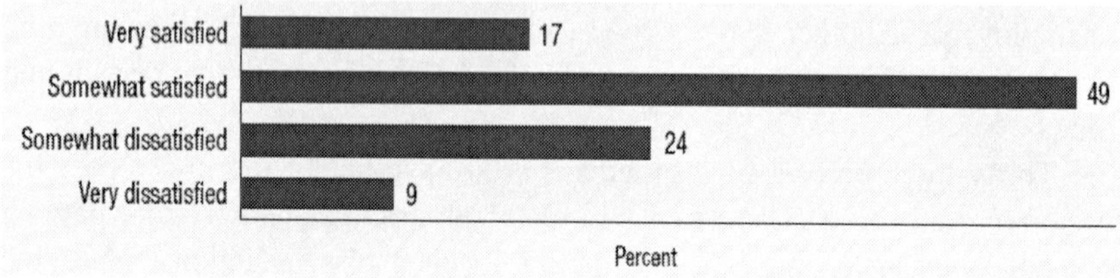

Note: Number of responses is 1,293.

Figure 8. Most respondents are satisfied with current job arrangements; Respondent satisfaction with their job arrangement.

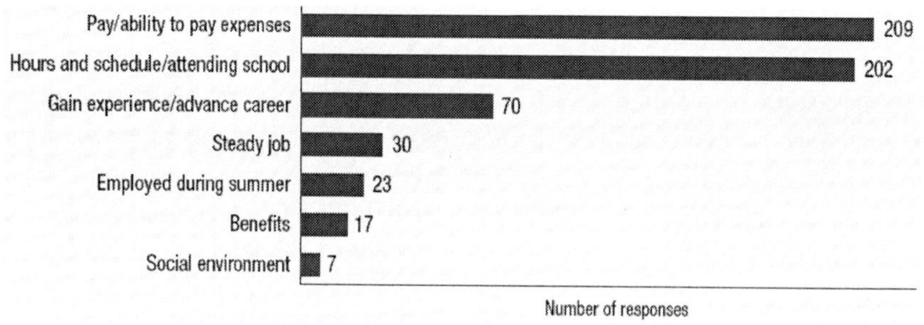

Figure 9. Job satisfaction is driven by compensation and schedule; In their own words,why respondents are satisfied with their job arrangements (data from unstructured responses).

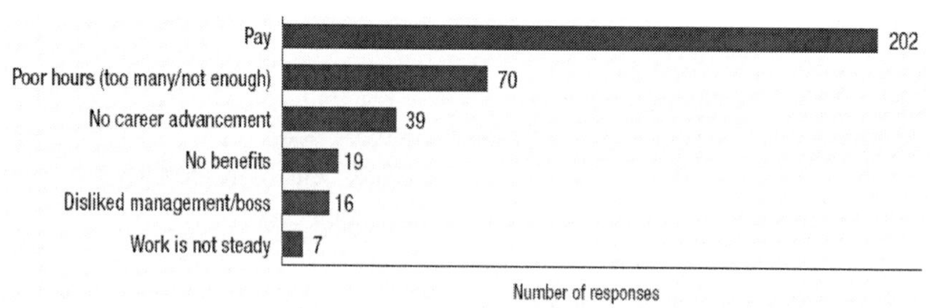

Figure 10. Lack of job satisfaction is driven by compensation and schedule; In their own words,why respondents are dissatisfied with their job arrangements (data from unstructured response.

UPWARD MOBILITY

As young people enter the workforce, they may be accepting a job to simply make ends meet or trying to establish a career path with future payoffs and upward mobility. The characteristics of early jobs often have long-lasting effects on job opportunities and growth. Research shows that young people that do not get a strong foothold in the job market typically maintain a below median wage throughout their careers.[27]

In the changing labor market, it is often difficult to determine the paths for upward mobility. For example, young workers, like their older counterparts, are increasingly acting as their own agents of employment with multiple firms, rather than as employees of a particular firm. While these arrangements allow many workers the opportunity to negotiate the terms of their employment, it reduces economic stability for many households, particularly low-wage workers. As the relationship between employers and workers shifts, employers may be less likely to provide traditional salaries and benefits to workers. And the opportunities to build a career under these conditions are unclear.

In the Survey of Young Workers, 54 percent of working respondents hold a "traditional job" (defined as a permanent, full-time job). The survey reveals that traditional jobs are associated with positive outcomes including greater optimism about the labor market, higher pay, and upward mobility.

Job versus Career

In 2012, the Heldrich Center's Work Trends surveys revealed that approximately one-fourth of recent college graduates reported they have a career, and nearly one-half reported their job is a stepping stone to a career.[28] The remainder reported their current job allows them to make ends meet. Recent high school graduates without a postsecondary degree were more likely to report their jobs are a stepping stone to a career or just to get them by.[29]

In the Survey of Young Workers, respondents also differentiated between careers that offer upward mobility and jobs that help them get by. Twenty-five percent of respondents with paid employment described their job as a "career," 35 percent described their job as a "stepping stone to a career," and 37 percent described their job as "just a job."

In the Survey of Young Workers, workers with a postsecondary degree have the most opportunity for upward mobility through a career. Within this educated group, 39 percent of respondents describe their current employment as a career, while 23 percent describe their current employment as "just a job" (figure 11). Respondents who are working while enrolled in a degree program are the least likely to have a "career" (9 percent).

Working respondents who lack postsecondary degrees have less upward mobility through a career. For example, those without a postsecondary degree and who are not currently enrolled in school are more likely to have a job (47 percent) and less likely to have a career (18 percent).

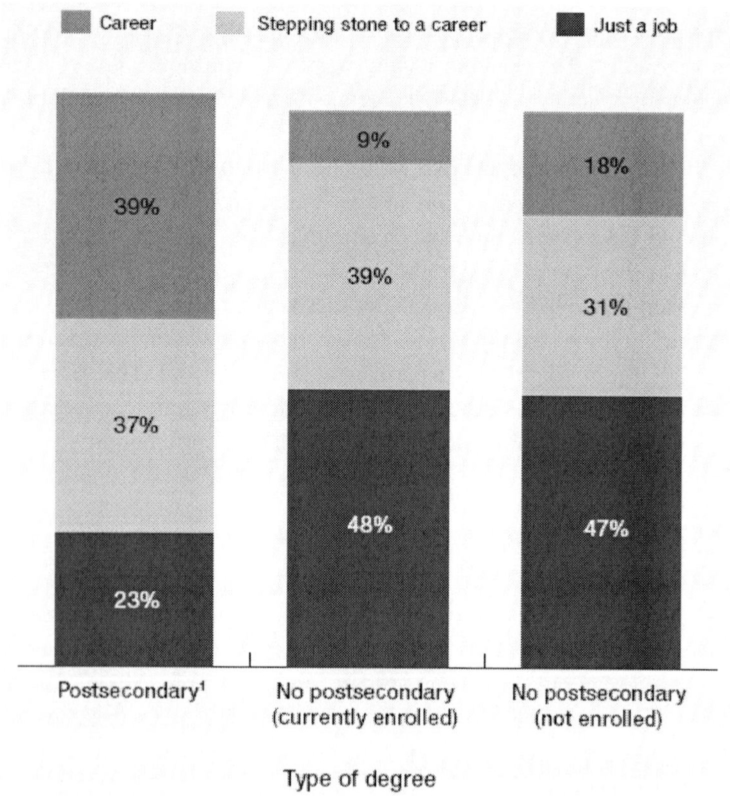

1. Includes associate's, bachelor's, master's, professional, and/or doctorate degree.

Note: Number of responses "postsecondary degree" is 743; "no postsecondary degree (currently enrolled)" is 209; and "no postsecondary degree (not enrolled)" is 418.

Figure 11. Workers with a postsecondary degree have the most opportunity for upward mobility; Current job vs. career status.

Full-Time versus Part-Time Jobs

In the Survey of Young Workers, two-thirds of respondents with a paid job are working full time. Furthermore, 17 percent of full-time workers hold down two or more jobs. Full-time workers reported that they average 43 hours per week at the job. The respondents cluster around a 40-to-50-hour work week with a handful of outliers. This average number of hours worked includes individuals who have more than one job.

In the survey, 28 percent of respondents with a paid job are working only one part-time job. An additional 8 percent of the working respondents have two or more part-time jobs. Respondents with part-time jobs average 22 hours of work per week.[30] The distribution of hours worked is broadly laid out between 0 and 40 hours with no real central tendency.

The full-time workers are more likely to have had a promotion in the past year (54 percent) and to perceive opportunities for advancement in their job (55 percent) than part-time workers (38 percent and 31 percent, respectively). The part-time workers are more likely to be students (51 percent) than full-time workers (19 percent).

Underemployment

More than half (56 percent) of the part-time workers reported being underemployed; these respondents want to work more hours than they are currently offered.[31] Forty percent of part-time workers reported that they could only find part-time work, and 18 percent had their hours cut by their employer. The other half of part-time workers choose part-time jobs to support a lifestyle choice, such as attending school (54 percent), caring for family (23 percent), caring for children (16 percent), or health-related issues (8 percent).

Overall, nearly one-third of all working respondents would like additional hours of paid work; the primary reason for wanting more work is financial. Forty-three percent of respondents want more hours to cover their living expenses, 19 percent have debt, and 30 percent would like to increase their savings.

Respondents with less than a high school education reported the most need for additional hours, particularly to pay their living expenses. Respondents with a postsecondary degree are most likely to want more hours to pay off debt.

Permanent versus Temporary Jobs

Young workers entering the labor market are affected by an increase in the use of "contingent" work arrangements, characterized by contracted, part-time, temporary, and seasonal work. According to a 2011 study by the Heldrich Center, jobs for recent high school and college graduates tend to be temporary. The study found that 40 percent of recent college graduates had held more than one job since graduation. In this study, 40 percent had quit a job since graduation, while 12 percent reported being laid off.[32]

As a respondent's level of education increases so does their likelihood of having a permanent job. The National Longitudinal Survey of Youth 2013 found that jobs held by high school dropouts were more likely to end after one year or less than were jobs held by workers with more education.[33]

In the Survey of Young Workers, 71 percent of working respondents have a permanent job, 18 percent have a temporary position, and 10 percent are not sure of their work status.[34] Significantly more young respondents, those 18 to 24 years old, held temporary jobs than the older respondents of ages 25 to 30 years old, suggesting that permanent jobs are "earned" from age and job experience. Likewise, the oldest respondents were most likely to have been in a job for two or more years (66 percent) than those 18 to 21 years old (8 percent) or their 22- to-25-yearold peers (26 percent) (figure 12).

Respondents with permanent jobs are more likely to be full-time workers (76 percent) and not enrolled in school (77 percent). Respondents with temporary jobs are more likely to be part time (61 percent) and students (52 percent).

The Survey of Young Workers indicates that 26 percent of permanent employees have some college education, and 40 percent of temporary employees have some college education. Furthermore, 25 percent of permanent employees have a bachelor's degree, and 15 percent of temporary employees have a bachelor's degree. In addition, the survey found that 65 percent of respondents with a temporary job found work through their own search, and 17 percent used personal networks. Only 9 percent of temporary workers used a temporary staffing agency to find their current position.

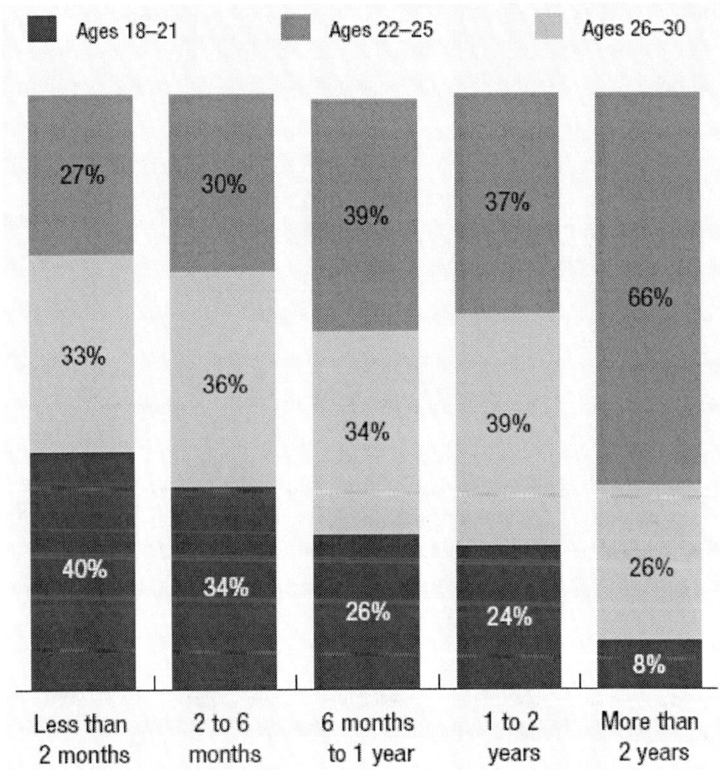

Note: Number of responses is 1,376.

Figure 12. Older respondents are more likely to have a steady job (two years or more).

While permanent work arrangements often offer a career path, most temporary positions do not. Thirty-two percent of permanent workers describe their job as a "career" compared with only 4 percent of temporary workers. Likewise, 35 percent of permanent workers believe their job is a "stepping stone to a career" compared with only 31 percent of temporary workers. Temporary work typically does not offer a developmental path with only 26 percent of temporary workers reporting that they have had a promotion compared with 57 percent of permanent workers. Finally, temporary workers are more likely to report that they are overqualified for their job (36 percent) than permanent workers (28 percent).

While 71 percent of working respondents have a permanent job, only half expect to stay at their job for more than one year and nearly one-fourth are not sure. Of those who plan to leave their job within one year, 19 percent reported that their job is temporary. Despite a challenging economic environment, 38 percent of those who expect to leave their job within one year expect to leave for another job.

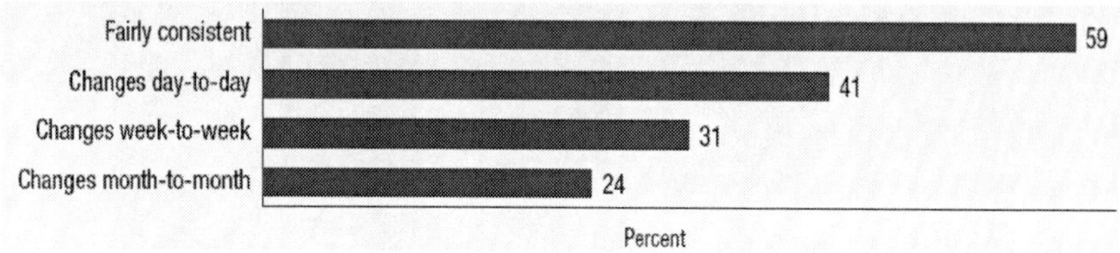

Note: Number of responses is 976.

Figure 13. A consistent schedule is associated with greater job satisfaction; Satisfied with work schedule.

A consistent schedule is associated with greater job satisfaction (figure 13). For example, 59 percent of workers with a consistent schedule are satisfied with their current job arrangements while only 24 percent of workers with a schedule that changes month-tomonth are satisfied with their current job arrangements.

Labor Market "Push Down"

According to the Economic Policy Institute's research in 2011, many young labor market entrants who take a job for which they are overqualified are motivated by financial need, since they cannot afford to wait out the economy's downturn. However, the loss or delay of human capital that occurs when a young graduate must take a job that does not use his or her acquired skills contributes to the long-run negative effect of recessions on the wages of young workers.[35]

According to a study by the Center for College Affordability and Productivity, while there are undoubtedly many who benefit from higher education, many Americans who obtain higher education do not achieve these economic gains.[36] This problem has been exacerbated because of job losses during the Great Recession. The study shows that the growth of supply of college-educated labor is exceeding the growth in the demand for such labor in the labor market.[37]

In the Survey of Young Workers, 62 percent of working respondents reported that they are "adequately qualified" for their current position. Full-time workers are more likely to report they are qualified (64 percent), and respondents who describe themselves as qualified are generally more optimistic (55 percent) than the sample as a whole.

The survey supports the theory that a lack of labor market opportunities pushed workers down the career ladder to jobs for which they are overqualified. First, 28 percent of working respondents reported that they are overqualified for their current job. Respondents with an associate's or bachelor's degree are most likely to report that they are overqualified for their job (30 percent and 35 percent, respectively). Respondents who reported they are overqualified for their jobs are more likely to be in full-time jobs (63 percent). Respondents who describe themselves as "overqualified" for their job are more likely to be pessimistic about the future (24 percent).

Second, 49 percent of those who are qualified for their job are working in a field related to their education, while only 32 percent of those who are over-qualified reported the same. These results suggest that some degree holders are being "pushed down" to jobs they are overqualified for by a lack of job opportunities.

Third, those who are overqualified typically view their job as "just a job" (55 percent) rather than a career builder compared with 37 percent of total workers. Even with their skills, they are less likely to see opportunities for advancement (42 percent) than the total population (45 percent).

Finally, those without a degree may be pushed down to unemployment. In the Survey of Young Workers, 83 percent of those seeking a job have not completed a postsecondary degree. More specifically, the unemployment rate for the survey sample is 18 percent.[38] In the survey, those without a postsecondary credential have an unemployment rate of 19 percent, while those with a postsecondary degree are experiencing unemployment at 10 percent. The national unemployment rate for 18- to 30-year-olds at the time the survey was administered was 18.7 percent.[39]

Respondents who reported they are overqualified for their job show many signs that they are working to improve their labor market prospects. For example, they are more open to moving for another job (66 percent) than total workers (56 percent). Furthermore, they are more likely to be enrolled in school (34 percent) or interested in enrolling in school (58 percent) than total workers (30 percent and 54 percent, respectively).

Upward Mobility

Despite the job push down, many working respondents have jobs with opportunities for advancement. Nearly half (49 percent) of working respondents have enjoyed a promotion at their current job. Full-time workers were much more likely to have earned a promotion (54 percent) than part-time workers (38 percent). Furthermore, 45 percent of all workers believe there is opportunity for advancement at their current job.

Financial Footing

About two-thirds of respondents (64 percent) are able to support their current household expenses with their household income. Although younger respondents were more likely to need financial assistance, age loses its significance when other demographic variables are included in the analysis. Survey findings show that being able to cover monthly household expenses is significantly affected by education, income, marital status, and having a paid job.

Although 64 percent can cover their monthly expenses, most of these respondents could not support themselves if they were temporarily out of work. Thirty-eight percent reported that they could support themselves without work for four weeks, and 24 percent would be able to support themselves without work for 12 weeks. As noted, respondents with higher levels of education are more likely to be able to support themselves if they are temporarily out of work.

Full-time workers are more likely to earn more and be financially self-sufficient than part-time workers (figure 14). Seventy-eight percent of full-time workers reported that they are able to cover their monthly household expenses compared with 52 percent of part-time workers. Sixty-six percent of workers who are not enrolled in school are able to cover their monthly expenses. Students, both full time and part time, were less able to cover their expenses (59 percent and 65 percent, respectively).

Workers with permanent jobs are more financially self-sufficient than those with temporary jobs. Respondents with permanent jobs are more likely to be able to cover their household expenses (76 percent) than those with temporary jobs (55 percent).

Those who are not able to cover their monthly household expenses were asked to describe, in their own words, "how they make ends meet." The largest number of respondents, 140, noted that they rely on their parents for assistance, while 63 respondents receive assistance from family members (without specifying parents) (figure 15). Fifty-five respondents reported that they take out loans of some nature, while a few reported that they rely on savings (20) or government assistance (16).

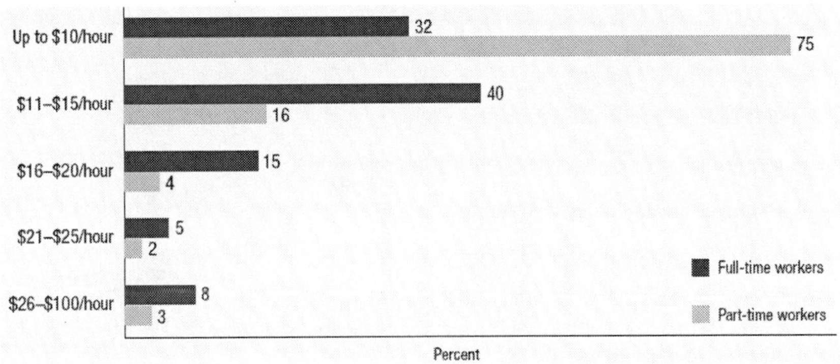

Note: Number of responses, "full-time workers" is 497; "part-time workers" is 317.

Figure 14. Full-time workers are more likely to earn higher hourly wages than part-time workers; Wages earned.

Furthermore, more than 40 percent of respondents currently receive assistance for rent and food from their parents or other family members. Thirty-eight percent of respondents receive assistance with miscellaneous bills such as the phone bill, and 30 percent of respondents receive assistance with health care.

Compensation

In the Survey of Young Workers, 71 percent of respondents with a paid job reported that they are paid an hourly wage, and 25 percent reported that they are paid a salary (figure 16). In addition, 41 percent of working respondents earn overtime pay, tips, or commissions at their job(s).

Since compensation is correlated with numerous demographic factors including age, regression analysis was used to control for these other characteristics. As it turns out, the significance of age on having an hourly, salary, or other type of pay decreases when adding in other demographic variables. Having an hourly wage is significantly affected by having a high school diploma or some college, compared with those having less than a high school diploma. In addition, earning a salary is significantly affected by having an associate's, master's, or other professional degree.

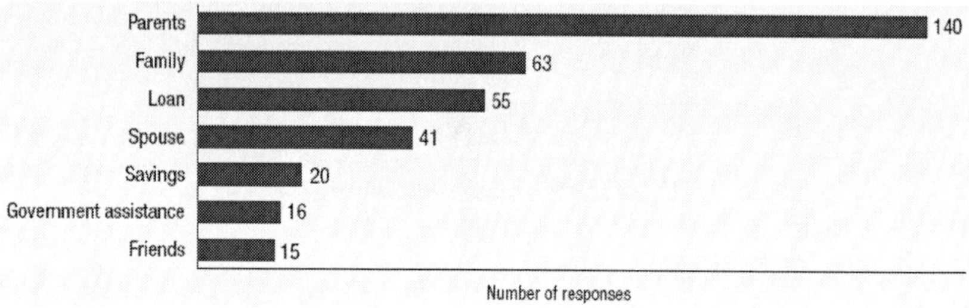

Note: Number of responses is 520.

Figure 15. Respondents who cannot cover their monthly housing expenses typically rely on their parents or other family members for assistance; In their own words, how respondents who cannot cover their monthly household expenses make ends meet (data from unstructured responses).

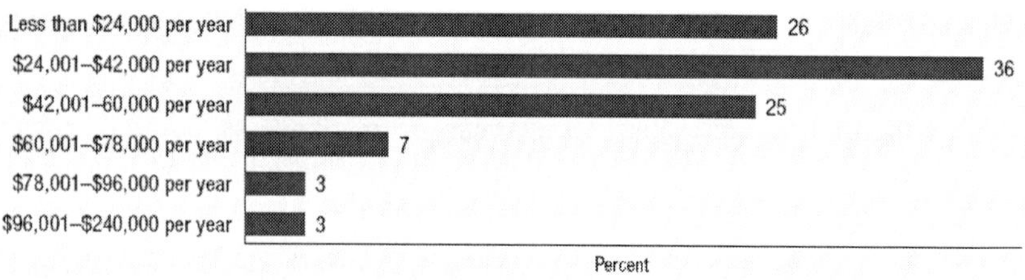

Note: Number of responses is 406.

Figure 16. Distribution of annual earnings of salaried workers in the survey; Annual earnings of salaried workers.

As such, respondents with higher levels of education are more likely to earn a salary than an hourly wage. The shift to a salary is most pronounced for respondents who have at least a bachelor's degree. More than 80 percent of respondents without a four-year degree earn an hourly wage, while 49 percent of those with a bachelor's degree, 70 percent of those with a master's degree, and 79 percent of those with a professional or doctorate degree earn a salary.

Interestingly, permanent workers are only marginally more satisfied with their level of pay. Fifty-two percent of permanent workers are satisfied or very satisfied with their income compared with 46 percent of temporary workers.

That said, permanent workers were far more satisfied with their benefits (49 percent) than temporary workers (16 percent).

Full-time students are more likely than part-time students to receive help from their parents to pay their bills including, living expenses, health care, car payments, educational loans, food, and miscellaneous bills than part-time students.

Salaries are more typical for traditional jobs and jobs that offer a career path. Most workers with a salary have a traditional job. Ninety-four percent of workers who earn a salary have a full-time job and 87 percent have a permanent job. Furthermore, 54 percent of respondents earning a salary describe their job as a career, while only 19 percent of full-time, hourly wage earners describe their job as a career.

Respondents who aligned their education and current work are more likely to have a higher salary as they begin their career. For example, respondents with higher salaries are more likely to have higher levels of education, to have received job information during colleges, and to have worked during the school year. Furthermore, respondents who are working in a field related to their education are more likely to have a higher salary.

Higher salaries and wages provide greater financial footing for full-time workers. Respondents with higher wages are more likely to be able to pay their monthly household expenses and to be able to stay financially afloat if they are out of work for four weeks. Furthermore, respondents with higher wages associate a greater value for the cost of their education.

Higher wages for full-time workers are correlated with other benefits including a "career" position rather than a "job," consistent work schedules, and training opportunities from employers. The respondents' level of satisfaction with their salary or wages is not correlated with the amount of their salary or wages. Rather, satisfaction is likely determined by qualitative factors including expectations.

In the survey, 41 percent of working respondents are satisfied with the benefits they currently receive from their employer, while 27 percent of working respondents are not satisfied with their current benefits. Twenty-nine percent are neither satisfied nor dissatisfied with their benefits. Respondents identified health care as the most important benefit to receive from an employer (figure 17). Seventy percent of these respondents have access to health care, and 65 percent of the working respondents have access to health care through their job. Finally, working respondents reported that paid sick leave or holidays is the second most important benefit to receive from their job. Fifty-three percent of working respondents currently have paid sick leave.

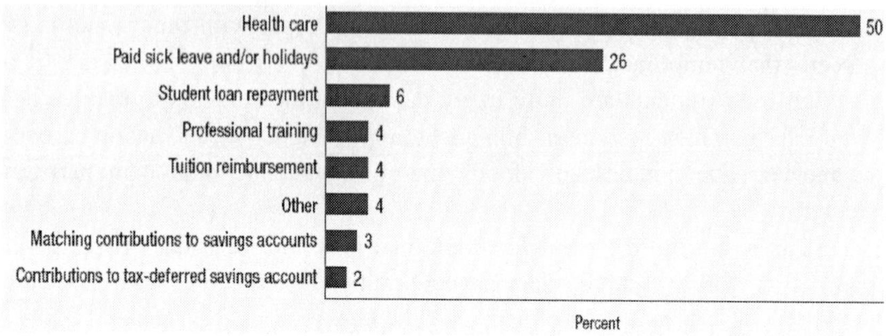

Figure 17. Working respondents report that health care is the most important benefit associated with a job; Most important benefit.

Young Workers' Unemployment

Since the Great Recession, college graduates continue to be employed at greater rates than high school graduates but at far lower rates than historical norms. Young college graduates typically have a strong labor market attachment; by attending and graduating college, they have made a significant down payment on their career in terms of time and money.[40] Yet at 85 percent, the employment-to-population ratio of young college graduates has significantly declined from the average of 89 percent over the 1990s business cycle and 87 percent over the 2000s business cycle.[41]

In the Survey of Young Workers, close to half (48 percent) of respondents who do not have a paid job are seeking paid employment and, therefore, unemployed. Some are not interested in engaging in a paid job because they are attending school (45 percent), caring for family and the home (20 percent), or self-employed (4 percent). Others face barriers to employment including disabilities (7 percent), health issues (3 percent), lack of skills and training (4 percent), lack of transportation (3 percent), or a lack of faith in the job market (1 percent).

In the Survey of Young Workers, although the average length of unemployment is 22 weeks, a few respondents who are experiencing very long periods of unemployment skewed the "typical" period of job seeking. The median duration of current unemployment is 10 weeks for the respondents. A relatively small number (10 percent) of unemployed respondents have been in the job search market for a year or more.

Some of the unemployed respondents are optimistic about their search, with 36 percent expecting to find a position in the next three months. A greater percent of job seekers (49 percent) are less optimistic, assuming it will take more than six months or an unknown amount of time to find a job. Only 20 percent of the job seekers had a job interview in the four weeks prior to completing the Survey of Young Workers.

Most of the unemployed respondents have low levels of educational attainment, including 83 percent who have not completed a postsecondary degree. Put another way, 32 percent of those with a high school diploma are unemployed compared with 10 percent of those with a bachelor's degree.

According to a 2012 study by the Heldrich Center, one in three high school graduates reported being unemployed and looking for work.[42] The findings reflect recent data from the BLS and Current Population Survey (CPS) that show an average jobless rate of 31 percent from April 2011 to March 2012. At the time of the Heldrich Center studies, those who graduated in the recession era were unemployed at a higher rate (37 percent) than those who graduated before the recession (23 percent).[43] In addition, nearly one in five high school graduates were working part time while looking for a full-time job.[44] The labor market demands recent job experience as well as education. In the Survey of Young Workers, respondents who lack experience, particularly recent experience, face difficulty finding a job. The greatest numbers of unemployed respondents are coming out of an educational setting (43 percent) or time caring for children or family members at home (24 percent), rather than a previous job. Only 17 percent of the unemployed respondents were most recently in another job. Unemployed respondents use multiple methods to job search including contacting employers directly (67 percent) and searching electronic job boards (64 percent). The unemployed also use personal networks, including family and friends (51 percent) and parents (36 percent) to search for jobs. Services from employment centers and schools are less popular options at 26 percent and 20 percent, respectively.

YOUNG WORKERS' OUTLOOK

Future Work Expectations

Today's young workers prepared for the workforce in the shadow of the Great Recession. As a result, there is clearly anxiety among young individuals when thinking about their job prospects. According to Pew's studies, from

1998 and 2009, "Young workers feel more vulnerable than they used to. In a 1998 survey, 65 percent of 18- to 34-year-olds working full time or part time said they were extremely or very confident that they could find another job if they lost or left their current job. The share of highly confident fell dramatically to 25 percent in 2009. It has rebounded somewhat since then (to 43 percent in the current survey) but is still nowhere near the 1998 level."[45]

In the Survey of Young Workers, 40 percent of respondents have held one, full-time job for the past year (figure 18). Another 13 percent have supplemented a full-time job with part-time work during the past year. Fourteen percent of respondents have held a single full-time job for the past five years. Another 30 percent have supplemented a full-time job with part-time work during the past five years. Some respondents have already held more than one full-time job. Six percent of respondents held more than one full-time job in the past year, and 26 percent held more than one full-time job in the past five years.

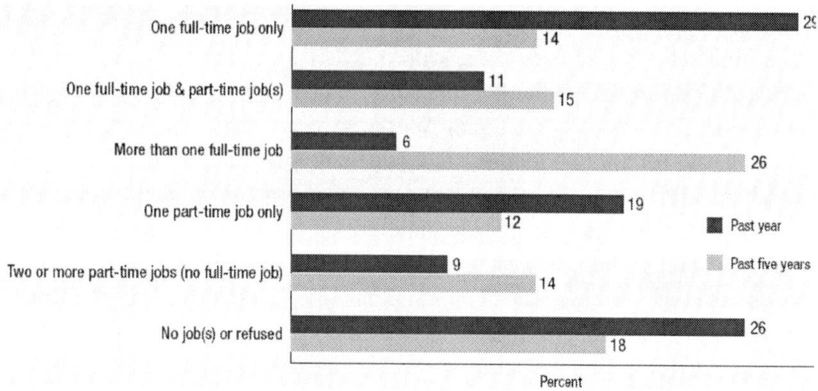

Note: Number of responses is 2,097.

Figure 18. Few workers have held a single full-time job for the past year or five years; Number of jobs held.

Many respondents reported working more than one job at a time. In fact, the number of respondents who work simultaneous jobs is increasing. Forty-seven percent of those who worked multiple jobs in the past year worked more than one job at the same time, while 38 percent of those who worked multiple jobs in the past five years worked more than one job at a time.

Many respondents who have worked more than one job in the past five years are satisfied (50 percent) or very satisfied (17 percent) with their work arrangements. Thirty-three percent of respondents who have worked more than one job in the past five years are dissatisfied with their work relationships. Interestingly, there is no correlation between satisfaction and whether an individual worked more than one job at the same time.

According to the survey, young workers expect greater job stability in the future (figure 19). Forty-four percent of respondents expect to hold a single full-time job in the next year. The survey showed that many young workers may have difficulty imagining five years in to the future as a nearly equal 43 percent expect to have a single, full-time job for the next five years. Only 3 percent expect to have multiple part-time jobs in the next five years.

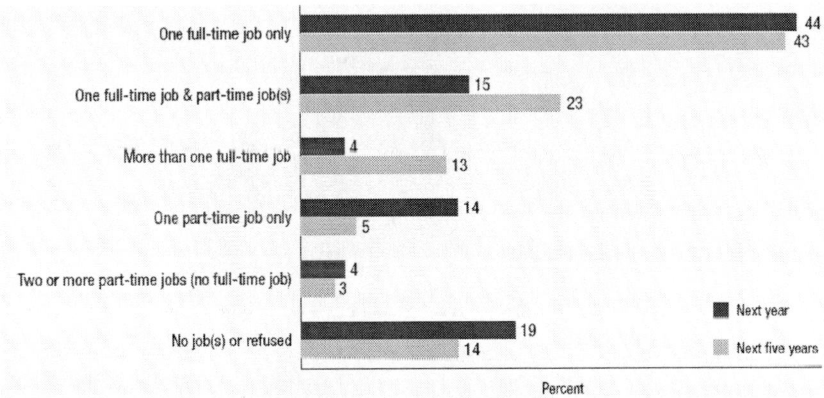

Note: Number of responses is 2,097.

Figure 19. Young workers expect greater job stability in the future; Number of jobs expecting to hold.

Those who expect to work more than one job also expect to manage more simultaneous jobs. Sixty-one percent of those who expect to work multiple jobs in the next year also expect to work more than one job at the same time, while 38 percent of those who expect to work multiple jobs in the next year do not expect to work more than one job at the same time.

Young Workers' Future Outlook

Although general optimism about the future has decreased since the Great Recession, young people continue to be more optimistic than the general population. According to a 2014 Gallup poll, 30 percent of Americans overall said it is a good time to find a quality job, while 46 percent of respondents ages 18 to 29 reported that this is a good time to find a quality job. The latest Gallup report continues a positive trend on this indicator for the overall population since reaching a low point of 8 percent in 2011. The recent numbers have not reached the pre-recession level of 2007 when 48 percent of the population reported it to be a good time to find a quality job.[46]

Likewise, respondents to the Survey of Young Workers are generally optimistic about the future. Comparable with the Gallup poll, 45 percent of survey respondents are optimistic about their future job opportunities compared with 21 percent who are pessimistic (figure 20). The remaining 34 percent are not sure about their future job opportunities.

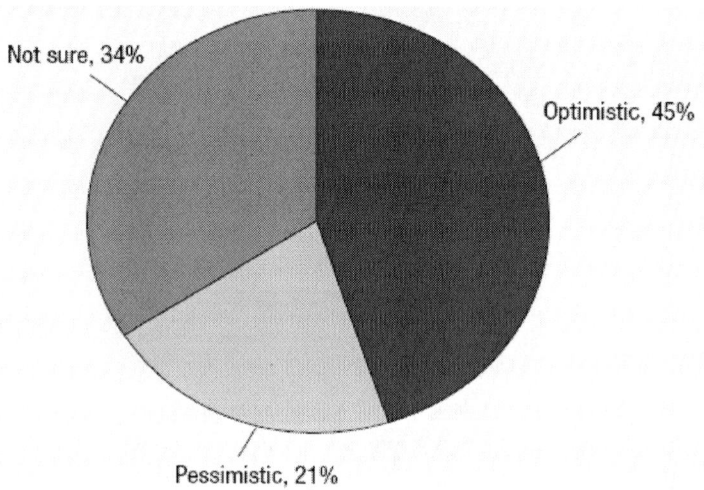

Note: Number of responses is 2,097.

Figure 20. Young workers are generally optimistic; Respondents' outlook.

The Impact of Education, Job Experience, and Income on Optimism

Optimistic respondents were asked to describe, in their own words, what makes them feel optimistic about their job futures. These respondents most commonly attributed their positive outlook to their level of education or their field of study (figure 21).

> What makes me feel optimistic about a future job is that I'm in school studying and learning the field. I will also intern before I graduate so I can ensure that I am fully ready.
>
> The field Iam in is always in high demand. I have a college degree so Ifeel confident I couldfind another job if something were to happen with my current job, however Iam confident I will keep my current job for a while.

Another sizable group of optimistic respondents attributed their outlook to their work experience or job market opportunities.

> I believe that with my accrued experience in medical device assembly, there may be other opportunities to expand in this area in the future. There are at least two other larger medical device companies in the area I live around.
>
> Economy is slowly recovering, and Boston has plenty of white-collar jobs for people with financial background.

As the Survey of Young Workers has revealed, education has a critical impact on young workers. The survey data show that respondents' optimism about their future goes hand-in-hand with higher levels of education. For example, 35 percent of respondents with a high school education, 59 percent with a bachelor's degree, and 68 percent with a professional or doctorate degree are optimistic about their job future. Being enrolled in an education program has an impact as well, as 57 percent of current students are optimistic about their job future. In addition, being enrolled full time is associated with greater rates of optimism (59 percent) than being enrolled part time (51 percent).

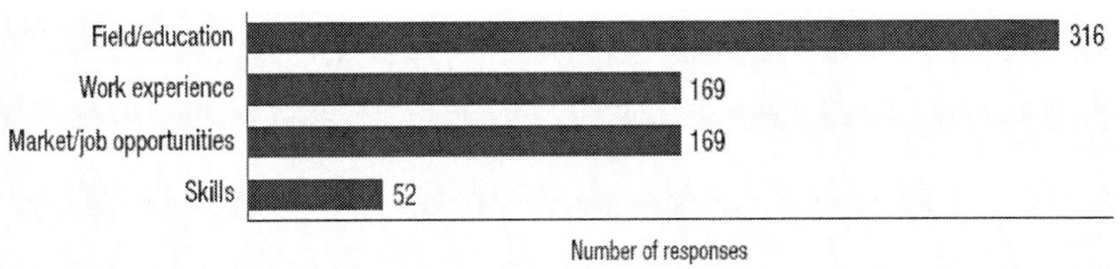

Note: Number of responses is 833.

Figure 21. Optimistic respondents often attribute their outlook to their level of education or field of study; In their own words,why respondents are optimistic about future job opportunities (data from unstructured responses).

Because education is correlated with numerous other factors that may affect a respondent's optimism about the labor market, regression analysis was used to control for these other characteristics. The regression analysis confirmed that being "optimistic" is significantly affected by level of education, having a paid job, and income.

Respondents who obtained early job experience during their schooling reported higher levels of optimism than those who did not hold a job prior to completing school. More specifically, respondents who held paid jobs during high school or college are more optimistic (51 percent and 55 percent, respectively) about their own future than those who lacked this job experience (37 percent and 42 percent, respectively).

Furthermore, respondents who are currently working a paid job are more likely to be optimistic about their job future (51 percent) than those who are not employed (35 percent). Likewise, respondents with a full-time, permanent job are more likely to be optimistic than those with a part-time or contingent job. Respondents with full-time jobs are more optimistic (54 percent) than those with part-time jobs (47 percent). Respondents with permanent jobs are more optimistic about their future (56 percent) than respondents working temporary positions (45 percent).

Respondents who used their education to help define a career path are more optimistic than other respondents. For example, respondents who reported working in a field closely related to their education are more optimistic (66 percent) than respondents who are not (42 percent). Furthermore, respondents who view their job as a "stepping stone to a career" or a "career" are more optimistic (52 percent and 71 percent, respectively) than respondents who view their employment as "just a job" and those who do not see "opportunities for advancement" (37 percent and 41 percent, respectively).

As noted, the respondents' optimism also increases with their salary and wages. Respondents who are satisfied with their current compensation are more likely to be optimistic (65 percent) about their future. Respondents who are able to cover their monthly household expenses (52 percent) as well as those who reported they could cover their expenses if out of work for four weeks (64 percent) are more optimistic than those who are not able to cover their expenses.

The Impact of Economic Opportunity on Pessimism

Respondents who are pessimistic or unsure about their job opportunities were also asked to describe, in their own words, what makes them feel this way. A lack of opportunity in the economy, a lack of job experience, and a lack of education caused these respondents the greatest amount of concern (figure 22).

> Iam currently studying in the business field. With the unemployment rate being high for a moment. I don't expect to quickly find a job with so many people graduating in the same year.
>
> I don't have a college degree, and even those people I know with them are largely unemployed or in service jobs like mine.
>
> So many employers require past experience, but being a college grad means I don't have any experience yet. How am I supposed to get experience if I can't get a job?

The regression analysis noted above also revealed that being "pessimistic" is significantly, adversely affected by the respondent's race, being in the wealthiest income bracket, marital status, and having a paid job. (Box 3 briefly discusses the effect of geography.)

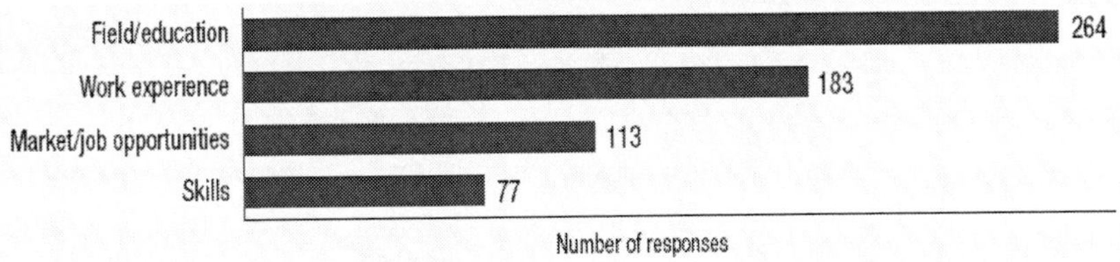

Note: Number of responses is 853.

Figure 22. Pessimistic respondents often attribute their outlook to economic conditions, a lack of education, and a lack of job experience; In their own words,why respondents are pessimistic about their future job opportunities (data from unstructured responses).

Importance of Steady Employment

Overall, young workers prefer steady employment (67 percent) to higher pay (30 percent) when seeking and selecting a job. In particular, respondents with work experience prefer steady pay and are developing a career. Respondents who held a paid job during high school are more likely to prefer steady pay (72 percent), as are those who held a paid job during college (70 percent). In addition, respondents that are working in their field of study are more likely to prefer steady employment (70 percent). Furthermore, respondents who are in a "career" or a "steppingstone-to-a-career" job prefer steady employment (71 percent). Those who have had a promotion in the past year with a pay increase (71 percent) or see the potential for a promotion (70 percent) prefer steady employment.

Box 3. Residents of Non-metropolitan Areas Reported Less Positive Labor Market Conditions than Residents of Metropolitan Areas

In the Survey of Young Workers, respondents living in non-metropolitan areas reported less positive labor market conditions than those residing in metropolitan areas. Respondents who live in non-metropolitan areas are more likely to be pessimistic about their job future. Furthermore, part-time workers in non-metropolitan areas are less confident about finding full-time work than those in metropolitan areas. Finally, working respondents in non-metropolitan areas are more likely to report they have "just a job" than a career.

That said, non-metropolitan respondents reported some labor market upsides. For example, these respondents are more likely to have gained job experience in high school.

A small number of characteristics define the 30 percent of respondents who prefer higher pay. Only the youngest respondents, those under 21 years of age with minimal exposure to the labor market, prefer higher pay (38 percent). Likewise, respondents with a less defined career path and who are less financially stable are more likely to prefer higher pay. Furthermore, respondents who describe their work as "just a job" (35 percent), rather than a career, are more likely to prefer higher pay than steady employment.

In addition, respondents with less stable financial conditions are more likely to prefer higher pay than their counterparts. For example, respondents who earn hourly pay (32 percent) are more likely to prefer higher pay. Respondents who currently receive parental assistance in the form of rent (32 percent), educational loans (33 percent), and health care (35 percent) are more likely to prefer higher pay. Respondents who would prefer to be working more hours (35 percent) and those who are dissatisfied with their work schedule (43 percent) are more likely to prefer higher pay.

A Pew study conducted from 1998 to 2009 found that "young workers feel more vulnerable than they used to." In 1998, the survey found 65 percent of 18- to 34-year-olds working full time or part time said they were extremely or very confident that they could find another job if they lost or left their current job. By 2009, the share highly confident fell dramatically to 25 percent. Currently, according to Pew, this figure has rebounded to 43 percent but is still nowhere near the 1998 level.[47]

Interestingly, Pew also found that "for young adults, bad times don't trump optimism. Among those age 18 to 34, nearly 9 in 10 (88 percent) say they either have or earn enough money now or expect they will in the future. Only 9 percent say they don't think they will ever have enough to live the life they want. Adults ages 35 and older are much less optimistic as 28 percent say they don't anticipate making enough money in the future. While young people are less likely now than they were before the recession to say they currently have enough income, their level of optimism is undiminished from where it was in 2004."[48]

POLICY AND RESEARCH IMPLICATIONS

The Survey of Young Workers provides some insights into the experiences of young workers, while raising questions about others. The findings described in this report are intended to help frame future discussion among experts on this topic.

The survey highlights the association between postsecondary education and positive labor market outcomes, ranging from optimism about one's job future to higher earnings. Hence, it is critical that young workers receive appropriate information that enables them to select an educational program that maximizes their job opportunities. Young adults considering postsecondary education must choose from a range of public, nonprofit, and for-profit institutions offering an assortment of degrees and training programs. However, limited information is available to young workers regarding the likelihood of being hired or the expected salary from these alternative options. The decision is further complicated for the majority of potential students who do not have the personal resources to pay for their education upfront or lack the ability to earn a full scholarship.

Because education plays such an important role in a young person's career opportunities, additional research on the outcomes from various educational paths is essential. School teachers, counselors, and other providers of career information also need these valuable resources to properly advise individuals as they develop a career path.

The importance of education also underscores the need to align educational opportunities with labor market demand. Creating channels of communication that allow educational institutions to better meet the needs of a changing labor market will provide better opportunities for young workers as well as employers. Furthermore, aligning education more closely with careers promotes student success, as people with some sense of where they are going are more likely to get there.[49]

The Survey of Young Workers results suggest that age is an important factor when considering a young workers' job status, compensation, and outlook on their own job future. This finding is not surprising: As the demand for postsecondary education increases, the on-ramp from education to full-time careers and family formation is delayed for many young adults.[50] In other words, many young workers are spending more time in education and training programs, which delays their entry into the labor market compared with previous generations.

Young workers are facing substantial financial challenges today that may have lasting effects. Later entry into the workforce has increased the age at which young workers reach the median wage from 26 to 30 in the past decade.[51] This effect has combined with other financial challenges for young workers, including delayed job opportunities because of the Great Recession and increased student debt. The implications of these statuses may be long-lasting.

The Survey of Young Workers is intended to provide a general overview of individuals at the onset of their workforce experience. The report highlights some notable differences based on respondent characteristics such as race and ethnicity, gender, and geographic location. These preliminary findings and the policy solutions that seek to address them merit additional analysis. While the survey adds to the body of knowledge provided by previous surveys and research on this topic, much remains to be explored. The Federal Reserve intends for this report to help shape future inquiry among workforce researchers, policy-makers, and practitioners. To this end, the Federal

Reserve will make the survey's data available to the public. In addition, the Federal Reserve will encourage additional use of these data for research both within the Federal Reserve System and among external parties.

APPENDIX A: METHODOLOGY

In order to create a nationally representative probability-based sample, GfK's KnowledgePanel has selected respondents based on both random digit dialing and address-based sampling (ABS). Since 2009, new respondents have been recruited using ABS.

To recruit respondents, GfK (formerly Knowledge Networks) sends out mailings to a random selection of residential postal addresses. Out of 100 mailings, approximately 14 households contact GfK and express an interest in joining the panel. Of those who contact GfK, three-fourths complete the process and become members of the panel. If the person contacted is interested in participating but does not have a computer or Internet access, GfK provides him or her with a laptop and Internet access. Panel respondents are continuously lost to attrition and added to replenish the panel, so the recruitment rate and enrollment rate may vary over time.

For the Survey of Young Workers, the number of KnowledgePanel members who were invited to complete the survey, and the invitation response rates, are presented in the introduction. A total of 4,242 e-mail solicitations to participate in the survey were sent out to a random selection of KnowledgePanel respondents, and data collection was terminated when the quota of 2,000 individuals completed the survey fully (a "completion rate" yield of 49 percent). To enhance the completion rate, an automatic e-mail reminder was sent to all nonresponding panel members in the sample after three days.

As with any survey method, probability-based Internet panel surveys are subject to potential survey error, such as noncoverage and nonresponse, due to the panel recruitment methods and to panel attrition. In order to address these potential sources of error, a poststratification adjustment is applied based on demographic distributions from the CPS. The variables used include gender, age, race/ethnicity, education, census region, residence in a metropolitan area, and access to the Internet.

The panel demographic poststratification weight is applied prior to a probability proportional to size selection of a study sample from KnowledgePanel. This weight is designed for sample selection purposes.

Once the sample has been selected and fielded, and all the study data are collected and made final, a poststratification process is used to adjust for any survey nonresponse as well as any noncoverage or under- and oversampling resulting from the study specific sample design.

Demographic and geographic distributions for the noninstitutionalized, civilian population ages 18 and over from the most recent CPS are used as benchmarks in this adjustment.

Comparable distributions are calculated by using all completed cases from the field data. Using the base weight as the starting weight, this procedure adjusts the sample data back to the selected benchmark proportions. Through an iterative convergence process, the weighted sample data are optimally fitted to the marginal distributions.

After this final poststratification adjustment, the distribution of the calculated weights are examined to identify and, if necessary, trim outliers at the extreme upper and lower tails of the weight distribution. The poststratified and trimmed weights are then scaled to the sum of the total sample size of all eligible respondents.

There are a few reasons that a probability-based Internet panel was selected as the method for this survey rather than an alternative survey method. The first reason is that these types of Internet surveys have been found to be representative of the population.[52] The second reason is that the ABS Internet panel allows the same respondents to be re-interviewed in subsequent surveys with relative ease, as they remain in the panel for several years.

The third reason is that Internet panel surveys have numerous existing data points on respondents from previously administered surveys, including detailed demographic and economic information. This allows for the inclusion of additional information on respondents without increasing respondent burden. Lastly, collecting data through an ABS Internet panel survey is cost effective and can be done relatively quickly.

APPENDIX B: RESPONSES TO THE SURVEY OF YOUNG WORKERS

The question numbers noted here correspond to the numbering in the survey database. Although some numbers have been skipped or reordered, it is important to keep the numbering consistent for future database users.

Table B.1. How would you describe employment opportunities for people like you who may be looking for work in the area where you live?

Response	Percent
Refused	0.7
Excellent	7.2
Good	31.6
Fair	37.8
Poor	22.8

Note: Number of responses is 2,097.

Table B.2. Would you say your expectations about future job opportunities are:

Response	Percent
Refused	0.3
Optimistic	44.8
Pessimistic	21.4
Not sure	33.5

Note: Number of responses is 2,097.

Table B.3. What is the highest level of formal education you have completed?

Response	Percent
Less than high school	10.2
High school diploma or the equivalent GED	29.0
Some college, no degree	29.5
Associate degree	8.5
Bachelor's degree	16.5
Master's degree	3.8
Professional or Doctorate degree	1.2
Other: Specify	1.3

Note: Number of responses is 2,097.

Table B.4. Are you currently working as a paid employee?

Response	Percent
Yes	59.7
No	40.3

Note: Number of responses is 2,097.

Table B.5. Are you currently employed full-time? That is, do you typically work 35 hours or more per week at one job?

Response	Percent
Yes	66.7
No	33.3

Note: Number of responses is 1,386.

Table B.6A. How many paid jobs of each type do you have? Number of full-time jobs:

Response	Percent
Refused	1.8
0	34.4
1	62.8
2	0.5
3	0.2
4	0.3

Note: Number of responses is 1,386.

Table B.6B. How many paid jobs of each type do you have? Number of part-time jobs:

Response	Percent
Refused	17.3
0	39.1
1	35.2
2	6.1
3	1.4
4	0.3
5	0.2
6	0.3
10	0.1

Note: Number of responses is 1,386.

Table B.7. For your main job, that is the job where you work the most hours, what type of of organization are you employed by?

Response	Percent
Refused	1.5
Government	12.8
For profit	72.6
Non-profit	13.1

Note: Number of responses is 1,386.

Table B.7A. Is your main job—that is, the job where you work the most hours—permanent or temporary?

Response	Percent
Refused	0.9
Permanent	71.0
Temporary	17.9
I don't know	10.2

Note: Number of responses is 1,386.

Table B.7B. How did you find your main job?

Response	Percent
Refused	3.0
I searched on my own	65.4
I used a temporary staffing agency	8.5
Other: Specify	23.1

Note: Number of responses is 354.

Table B.8A. Are you currently looking for a paid job?

Response	Percent
Yes	47.5
No	52.5

Note: Number of responses is 711.

Table B.9 is omitted.

Table B.10. Which one of the following best describes the main reason you are not looking for a paid job?

Response	Percent
Refused	1.9
I am self employed	4.3
I believe there is no work available for me	1.3
I need education/training to get a job	3.7
I am a student	45.3
I don't need or want a job	4.8
I have health problems	3.3
I need transportation to get to and from work	3.2
Other: Specify	3.9
I am a homemaker/caring for family	20.2
I am disabled	7.3
I believe the work available does not pay enough to be worthwhile	0.9

Note: Number of responses is 371.

Table B.11. Do you currently:

Response	Percent
Refused	0.8
Own a business	4.3
Run a non-profit enterprise	1.5
Neither	93.4

Note: Number of responses is 2,097.

Table B.11A. Does anyone in your immediate family own a business or run a nonprofit enterprise?

Response	Percent
Refused	0.4
Yes	13.2
No	79.1
I don't know	7.2

Note: Number of responses is 2,097.

Table B.12. Do you currently earn any money from activities where you are "your own boss"?

Response	Percent
Refused	0.9
Yes	9.7
No	89.4

Note: Number of responses is 2,097.

Table B.13. Do you currently have an unpaid job, such as an internship or a volunteer position?

Response	Percent
Refused	1.0
Yes	10.7
No	88.3

Note: Number of responses is 2,097.

Tables B.14 and B.15 are omitted.

Table B.16. How are you paid at your main job (the job where you currently work the most hours)?

Response	Percent
Refused	0.8
Hourly wage	70.5
Salary	24.5
Other	4.2

Note: Number of responses is 1,386.

Table B.17 is omitted.

Table B.18A. As a household, are you able to cover monthly expenses with your current household income?

Response	Percent
Refused	1.4
Yes	64.3
No	34.3

Note: Number of responses is 2,097.

Table B.18B is omitted.

Table B.18C. Did you incur debt to pay for any portion of your education or training?

Response	Percent
Refused	1.3
Yes	33.5
No	65.2

Note: Number of responses is 2,097.

Table B.18D. Please check off any of the following things that your parents or other family members help you with financially:

Response	Percent
Living situation (such as mortgage, rent, or just living with parents or relatives)	47.9
Healthcare costs	29.8
Food	43.2
Miscellaneous bills (such as cell phone bills)	38.0
Car payment	15.6
Education loans	14.6
Savings	6.6
Other	4.8
Refused	28.3

Note: Number of responses is 2,097.

Table B.19. Would you be willing to relocate to another community in order to obtain a job or advance your career?

Response	Percent
Refused	1.0
Yes	53.7
No	17.0
I don't know	28.3

Note: Number of responses is 2,097.

Table B.20. Do you believe you now have the level of education and training needed for the type of job that you would like to hold in the next 5 years?

Response	Percent
Refused	1.2
Yes	36.6
No	44.3
I don't know	17.9

Note: Number of responses is 2,097.

Table B.21. Are you currently enrolled in an education or training program?

Response	Percent
Refused	1.3
Yes	31.6
No	67.1

Note: Number of responses is 2,097.

Table B.22. Are you enrolled full time or part time?

Response	Percent
Refused	0.4
Full time	73.4
Part time	26.2

Note: Number of responses is 648.

Table B.23. What type of certification or degree program are you enrolled in?

Response	Percent
Refused	0.1
High school diploma or the equivalent GED	12.6
Certificate or vocational program	6.7
Associate degree	19.8
Bachelor's degree	43.7
Master's degree	7.4
Professional or doctorate degree	6.4
Other: Specify	3.2

Note: Number of responses is 648.

Table B.24. How are you financing your current education or training program?

Response	Percent
I am paying with loans	41.2
My parents or family members are paying with cash	29.9
I received an academic scholarship	29.7
I am paying with cash	17.1
My parents are paying with loans	8.8
My employer is paying	8.0
Other grants or scholarships	7.2
Other grants or scholarships	3.4
Refused	1.2

Note: Number of responses is 648.

Table B.24A is omitted.

Table B.24B. How would you say the lifetime financial benefits of your most recent educational program compare to the financial costs of this education?

Response	Percent
Refused	2.6
The financial benefits are MUCH LARGER than the costs	19.6
The financial benefits are SOMEWHAT LARGER than the costs	15.6
The financial benefits are ABOUT THE SAME as the costs	12.1
The financial benefits are SOMEWHAT SMALLER than the costs	7.5
The financial benefits are MUCH SMALLER than the costs	7.2
I don't know	35.4

Note: Number of responses is 2,097.

Table B.25. Are you interested in obtaining additional education or training?

Response	Percent
Refused	2.4
Yes	50.7
No	24.9
I don't know	22.0

Note: Number of responses is 1,449.

Table B.26. Seeing as you may be interested in additional education or training, please indicate whether each of following reasons describes why you are not enrolled:

Response	Percent
I don't want to borrow money to enroll	62.7
I can't afford to enroll	57.7
I am concerned that even after the program, I will not land a job in my field of interest	44.4
I don't know which program will improve my job opportunities	39.4
The schedule does not work for me	34.2
I don't know where to enroll	26.1
I am concerned that the program will be too challenging	19.2
The program is not offered at my local institutions	18.6
I don't meet the requirements to enroll	15.8

Note: Number of responses is 1,053.

Table B.27. During high school, did you work for pay?

Response	Percent
Refused	1.3
Yes	53.8
No	44.9

Note: Number of responses is 2,097.

Table B.28. During high school, did you receive information about jobs and careers?

Response	Percent
Refused	1.8
Yes	62.6
No	24.6
I don't know	11.0

Note: Number of responses is 2,097.

Table B.29. During high school, where did you obtain information about jobs and careers?

Response	Percent
Parent(s)	56.6
Friends and family	48.5
High school teacher or counselor	75.2
Online research	38.8
Employment service agency	6.5
A business where I worked	6.2
Other: Specify	3.0
Refused	2.0

Note: Number of responses is 1,387.

Table B.30. Did the information you received from your high school help you get a job?

Response	Percent
Refused	0.2
Yes	20.8
No	70.2
I don't know	8.8

Note: Number of responses is 1,032.

Table B.31. During college, did you work for pay?

Response	Percent
Refused	1.5
Yes	74.2
No	24.3

Note: Number of responses is 1,548.

Table B.32. During college, did you hold one or more unpaid internships?

Response	Percent
Refused	1.9
Yes	21.4
No	76.7

Note: Number of responses is 1,548.

Table B.33. During college, did you work or intern during the school year?

Response	Percent
Refused	0.9
Yes	62.5
No	36.7

Note: Number of responses is 1,286.

Table B.34. During college, did you receive information about jobs and careers?

Response	Percent
Refused	2.1
Yes	66.3
No	21.8
I don't know	9.8

Note: Number of responses is 1,548.

Table B.35. During college, where did you obtain information about jobs and careers?

Response	Percent
College professor or counselor	73.3
Online research	61.1
Friends and family	46.0
Parents	36.2
Employment services agency	19.2
Business where I worked	11.5
Other: Specify	6.9
Refused	0.9

Note: Number of responses is 1,090.

Table B.36. Did the information you received from your college help you get a job?

Response	Percent
Refused	0.8
Yes	39.9
No	46.7
I don't know	12.5

Note: Number of responses is 852.

Table B.37. Are you working in a career field that is closely related to your education and training?

Response	Percent
Refused	2.1
Yes	41.7
No	51.2
I don't know	5.0

Note: Number of responses is 1,386.

Table B.38. How qualified would you describe yourself for performing the tasks required of your main job (the job where you work the most hours)? Do you think you are…

Response	Percent
Refused	1.5
Overqualified	28.2
Adequately qualified	62.0
In need of additional training	8.4

Note: Number of responses is 1,386.

Table B.39. Do you consider your main job (the job where you work the most hours) to be a career, a stepping stone to a career, or just a job to get you by?

Response	Percent
Refused	2.9
Career	24.8
Stepping stone to a career	34.9
Just a job	37.4

Note: Number of responses is 1,386.

Table B.40. Please indicate whether you used each the following strategies to find your main job (the job where you work the most hours):

Response	Percent
I contacted the employer directly	67.1
Other family and friends provided a contact	26.5
Searched electronic job boards (e.g., Monster, CareerBuilder, Craigslist, Indeed)	20.6
My parent(s) provided a contact	13.7
Services from school teacher, professor, or counselor	9.7
Posted online resume/advertisement (e.g., LinkedIn, Twitter, Facebook, Craigslist)	8.8
Services from an employment center	8.4
Other: Specify	7.6

Note: Number of responses is 1,386.

Table B.41. Have you been promoted with a pay increase since you started your main job (the job where you work the most hours)?

Response	Percent
Refused	1.5
Yes	48.6
No	49.9

Note: Number of responses is 1,386.

Table B.42. Are there opportunities for advancement with a pay increase at your main job (the job where you work the most hours)?

Response	Percent
Refused	3.1
Yes	45.0
No	30.6
I don't know	21.3

Note: Number of responses is 671.

Table B.43. How quickly do you expect to be promoted?

Response	Percent
Within the next 6 months	20.6
Within next year	19.4
Within the next 2 years	15.8
In more than 2 years	8.4
I do not expect to be promoted	13.2
I don't know	22.5

Note: Number of responses is 310.

Table B.44 is omitted.

Table B.45. Compared to the number of hours you worked last week, would you prefer to work:

Response	Percent
Refused	2.5
Work more hours	31.3
About the same number of hours	51.8
Work less hours	14.4

Note: Number of responses is 1,386.

Table B.46. What is the main reason you are seeking more hours?

Response	Percent
Refused	0.4
To pay my living expenses	43.2
To pay off debt	19.3
To increase my savings	29.8
To gain more work experience	3.5
Other: Specify	3.7

Note: Number of responses is 352.

Table B.47. How satisfied are with your work schedule for your current job or jobs?

Response	Percent
Refused	2.5
Satisfied	49.8
Neither satisfied nor dissatisfied	34.6
Dissatisfied	13.1

Note: Number of responses is 1,386.

Table B.48. Is your work schedule for your job or jobs:

Response	Percent
Refused	2.4
Fairly consistent	65.1
Changes day-to-day	14.0
Changes week-to-week	15.9
Changes month-to-month	2.6

Note: Number of responses is 100.

Table B.49. Please indicate whether each of the following is a reason that you are currently working part time rather than full time:

Response	Percent
I prefer part-time work	47.8
My employer cut my hours due to business conditions	18.0
I could only find part-time work	40.1
I am enrolled in school/training program	54.1
I am caring for young children	15.9
I have family responsibilities	23.4
I have health problems	7.9
Other: Specify	5.0

Note: Number of responses is 410.

Table B.50. A year from now, do you expect to have a full-time job (35 hours or more per week) with a single employer?

Response	Percent
Refused	1.6
Yes	40.2
No	32.8
I don't know	25.4

Note: Number of responses is 410.

Table B.51. A year from now do you expect to be working full time (35 hours or more per week) but for more than one employer?

Response	Percent
Refused	1.8
Yes	9.4
No	60.2
I don't know	28.6

Note: Number of responses is 410.

Table B.52. How long have you been employed at your main job (the job where you work the most hours)?

Response	Percent
Refused	2.4
Less than 2 months	8.2
2 to 6 months	19.5
6 months to 1 year	15.4
1 to 2 years	18.6
More than 2 years	35.9

Note: Number of responses is 1,386.

Table B.53. Do you think you can continue to work at your main job as long as you wish?

Response	Percent
Refused	1.7
Yes	72.2
No	11.2
I don't know	14.9

Note: Number of responses is 1,386.

Table B.54. How long do you expect to be at your main job (the job where you work the most hours)?

Response	Percent
Refused	2.9
Less than 2 months	3.7
2 to 6 months	7.8
6 months to 1 year	10.2
1 to 2 years	18.8
More than 2 years	33.3
I don't know	23.3

Note: Number of responses is 1,386.

Table B.55. What is the most important reason you expect to leave your main job within a year?

Response	Percent
Refused	1.6
Job is temporary	19.3
Business conditions may cause my employer to cut back	1.5
New technology will eliminate my job	0.5
I want to be my own boss	3.4
I am moving	9.8
I will get another job	37.9
I will be attending school	12.3
Family responsibilities	4.4
I have health problems	1.3
Other: Specify	8.1

Note: Number of responses is 310.

Table B.56. If you had to choose, is it more important to have a job that pays more or a job that is more likely to provide steady employment?

Response	Percent
Refused	2.9
Higher pay	30.0
Steady employment	67.1

Note: Number of responses is 1,386.

Table B.57. Do you receive overtime pay, tips, or commissions from any of your paid jobs?

Response	Percent
Refused	2.4
Yes	40.8
No	56.8

Note: Number of responses is 1,386.

Table B.58. How satisfied are you with the total amount of salary or wages you earn from the paid job or jobs you now hold?

Response	Percent
Refused	2.2
Very satisfied	12.3
Somewhat satisfied	37.9
Neither satisfied nor dissatisfied	19.2
Somewhat dissatisfied	21.0
Very dissatisfied	7.3

Note: Number of responses is 1,386.

Table B.59A. If you were out of work for the next four weeks, would you able to pay your living expenses?

Response	Percent
Refused	2.6
Yes	38.2
No	47.8
I don't know	11.4

Note: Number of responses is 1,386.

Table B.59B. If you were out of work for the next three months, would you able to pay your living expenses?

Response	Percent
Refused	2.9
Yes	24.4
No	59.9
I don't know	12.8

Note: Number of responses is 1,386.

Table B.60. How satisfied are you with the benefits you currently receive from your employer or employers?

Response	Percent
Refused	2.6
Very satisfied	17.5
Somewhat satisfied	23.6
Neither satisfied nor dissatisfied	29.4
Somewhat dissatisfied	14.5
Very dissatisfied	12.5

Note: Number of responses is 1,386.

Table B.61. Do you receive paid time off for sick leave and/or holidays from any of your paid jobs?

Response	Percent
Refused	2.8
Yes	53.3
No	43.9

Note: Number of responses is 1,386.

Table B.62. Do you have health care from any source?

Response	Percent
Refused	2.7
Yes	70.2
No	27.1

Note: Number of responses is 1,386.

Table B.63. Do you receive this health care either through an employer or employment agency?

Response	Percent
Refused	0.2
Yes	65.5
No	34.3

Note: Number of responses is 1,056.

Table B.64. Does your employer pay for:

Response	Percent
Refused	0.5
All of your health care premium	23.4
Part of your health care premium	64.1
None of your health care premium	12.0

Note: Number of responses is 742.

Table B.65. Do you have training opportunities through an employer or employers?

Response	Percent
Refused	2.1
Yes	44.2
No	37.1
I don't know	16.6

Note: Number of responses is 1,386.

Table B.66 is omitted.

Table B.67. Are you a member of a labor union or an employee association similar to a union?

Response	Percent
Refused	2.0
Yes	6.7
No	85.0
I don't know	6.3

Note: Number of responses is 1,386.

Table B.68A. How many full-time jobs have you had in the past year?

Response	Percent
Refused	11.7
0	42.3
1	39.6
2	4.8
3	1.1
4	0.3

Note: Number of responses is 2,097.

Table B.68B. How many part-time jobs have you had in the past year?

Response	Percent
Refused	17.2
0	42.3
1	28.5
2	8.4
3	2.7
4	0.5
6	0.2

Note: Number of responses is 2,097.

Table B.68C. Did you work at more than one of these jobs at the same time?

Response	Percent
Refused	0.7
Yes	47.2
No	52.1

Note: Number of responses is 625.

Table B.69A. How many paid full-time jobs have you held in the past five years?

Response	Percent
Refused	11.0
0	33.9
1	29.8
2	15.1
3	6.6
4	2.2
5	1.0
6	0.4
7	0.1
10	0.1

Note: Number of responses is 2,097.

Table B.69B. How many paid part-time jobs have you held in the past five years?

Response	Percent
Refused	15.7
0	28.2
1	24.9
2	13.5
3	8.7
4	4.4
5	2.7
6	0.7
7	0.5
8	0.2
10	0.3
12	0.1

Note: Number of responses is 2,097.

Table B.69C. Did you work at more than one of these jobs at the same time?

Response	Percent
Refused	0.1
Yes	38.0
No	61.8

Note: Number of responses is 1,293.

Table B.69D. How satisfied are you with your full- and part-time job arrangements over the past five years?

Response	Percent
Refused	0.7
Very satisfied	16.6
Somewhat satisfied	49.2
Somewhat dissatisfied	24.2
Very dissatisfied	9.3

Note: Number of responses is 1,293.

Table B.70A. Looking to the future, approximately how many paid full-time jobs do you expect to have in the next year?

Response	Percent
Refused	12.5
0	24.8
1	59.3
2	2.2
3	0.8
4	0.2
5	0.2

Note: Number of responses is 2,097.

Table B.70B. Looking to the future, approximately how many paid part-time jobs do you expect to have in the next year?

Response	Percent
Refused	23.2
0	42.4
1	27.1
2	6.3
3	0.7
4	0.1
5	0.2
6	0.1

Note: Number of responses is 2,097.

Table B.70C. Do you expect to work at more than one of these jobs at the same time?

Response	Percent
Refused	0
Yes	61.5
No	38.4

Note: Number of responses is 510.

Table B.71A. Looking to the future, approximately how many paid full-time jobs do you expect to have in the next five years?

Response	Percent
Refused	10.0
0	11.8
1	65.8
2	9.1
3	2.3
4	0.7
5	0.4

Note: Number of responses is 2,097.

Table B.71B. Looking to the future, approximately how many paid part-time jobs do you expect to have in the next five years?

Response	Percent
Refused	27.0
0	38.3
1	23.7
2	7.0
3	2.1
4	0.4
5	0.8
6	0.4
8	0.1

Note: Number of responses is 2,097.

Table B.71C. Do you expect to work at more than one of these jobs at the same time?

Response	Percent
Refused	0.2
Yes	38.0
No	61.8

Note: Number of responses is 825.

Table B.72A. How much longer do you expect it to take you to find a paid job?

Response	Percent
Refused	3.5
Less than 2 months	21.9
2 to 3 months	14.2
3 to 6 months	11.9
More than 6 months	8.4
I don't know	40.1

Note: Number of responses is 340.

Table B.73. Please indicate whether you have used each of the following strategies to find a paid job:

Response	Percent
I searched electronic job boards (e.g., Monster, CareerBuilder, Craigslist, Indeed)	63.8
I contacted the employers directly	66.6
Other family and friends provided me with contacts	50.9
My parent(s) provided me with contacts	36.2
I posted a resume/advertisement (e.g., LinkedIn, Twitter, Facebook, Craigslist)	29.0
An employment center provided services	26.5
The school provided services from school teacher, professor, or counselor	20.2
Other: Specify	9.9

Note: Number of responses is 340.

Table B.74. Have you been interviewed for a job in the past four weeks?

Response	Percent
Refused	2.2
Yes	19.8
No	78.0

Note: Number of responses is 340.

Table B.75. Before you started this job search, what was the main thing you were doing?

Response	Percent
Refused	3.9
Attending school	42.5
Caring for family	24.1
Working	16.9
Military service	0.9
Other: Specify	11.7

Note: Number of responses is 340.

Table B.76. Why did you leave your last job?

Response	Percent
Refused	1.8
I was laid off	40.4
I quit	19.6
The job was temporary	23.0
I was fired	15.1

Note: Number of responses is 66.

Table B.77. Which statement best describes your self-employment enterprise?

Response	Percent
Refused	5.8
A part-time business to supplement other income	32.0
A start-up business with the potential to become my permanent, main source of income	27.5
A career that supplies my main source of income	25.0
Other: Specify	9.7

Note: Number of responses is 298.

Table B.78. Please indicate whether each of the following was a reason that you started your own business or became your own boss:

Response	Percent
I always wanted to be my own boss	63.7
I thought I could earn more money by having my own business	57.8
I had a great business idea	46.9
I thought my knowledge and skills were best suited to being an entrepreneur	46.4
I wanted to feel good about the contributions my work makes to society	43.8
I was inspired by a successful entrepreneur	43.1
Friends/relatives suggested that I become an entrepreneur	40.5
I had no other option to earn a living	30.4

Note: Number of responses is 298.

Table B.79 is omitted.

Table B.80. Which one of the following best describes how you came to own this enterprise?

Response	Percent
Refused	6.5
I started the business myself or with partners	42.6
I bought the business	18.2
Took over a family business	22.4
Other: Specify	10.3

Note: Number of responses is 111.

Table B.81. Are you the sole owner of this enterprise?

Response	Percent
Refused	7.0
Yes	48.8
No	44.2

Note: Number of responses is 111.

Tables B.82 and B.83 are omitted.

Table B.84. How many people does your business currently employ, including part time and temporary? (Do not include yourself or outside contractors.)

Response	Percent
Refused	15.3
0	27.1
1	16.4
2	10.2
3	9.7
4	9.3
5	5.0
6	3.1
10	0.1
14	1.8
20	1.5
25	0.1
40	0.2
87	0.2
342	0.1

Note: Number of responses is 111.

Table B.85. Please indicate whether each of the following sources of financing was used to fund the start of your business:

Response	Percent
Personal savings	73.7
Bank loan	30.4
Credit card	25.6
Government loan	24.9
Crowd funding	24.2
Loan from small business support organization	21.6
Gifts or loans from family and friends	13.2
Other: Specify	10.5

Note: Number of responses is 81.

Table B.86. Please indicate whether each of the following types of assistance was used to start or grow your business:

Response	Percent
Developing a business plan	28.9
Marketing assistance	24.4
Financial management	22.2
Legal guidance	21.0
Tax assistance	18.9
Assistance with Certifications	11.9
Other: Specify	8.6

Note: Number of responses is 298.

Table B.87. Do you have any interest in starting a business or "being your own boss" in the next five years?

Response	Percent
Refused	3.1
Yes	20.3
No	53.1
I don't know	23.5

Note: Number of responses is 1,799.

Table B.88. What is the main reason that best describes why you might want to start your own business?

Response	Percent
Refused	5.7
I wanted to be my own boss	30.3
I think I could earn more money by being my own boss	15.9
I have a great business idea	9.9
I want to feel good about the contributions my work makes to society	8.5
I think my knowledge and skills were best suited to being an entrepreneur	8.3
I am inspired by successful entrepreneurs	6.3
I have no other option to earn a living	4.7
Friends/relatives suggest that I become an entrepreneur	3.5
Other: Specify	6.9

Note: Number of responses is 100.

Table B.89. Please indicate whether each of the following reasons describes why you have not become your own boss:

Response	Percent
Lack of funding	79.0
Lack of knowledge about starting a business	67.6
Lack of network/business contacts	63.5
Too much risk	55.0
Fear of failure	46.7
Other: Specify	12.6

Note: Number of responses is 790.

Table B.90. Summary demographics

Demographic	Percent
Age	
18	7.1
19	6.7
20	7.7
21	7.5
22	9.0
23	7.8
24	8.1
25	6.4
26	6.5
27	9.8
28	7.2
29	6.9
30	9.3
Race/ethnicity	
White, non-Hispanic	57.1
Black, non-Hispanic	13.3
Other, non-Hispanic	7.0
Hispanic	20.4
2+ races, non-Hispanic	2.2

Gender	
Male	49.6
Female	50.4
Household head	
No	53.0
Yes	47.0
Marital status	
Married	21.0
Widowed	0.1
Divorced	2.0
Separated	0.8
Never married	62.5
Living with partner	13.7
MSA status	
Non-metro	13.3
Metro	86.7
Region	
Northeast	18.4
Midwest	20.8
South	35.9
West	24.9

Note: Number of responses is 2,097.

End Notes

[1] U.S. Department of Labor, Bureau of Labor Statistics (2014), Current Population Survey (CPS), *Unemployment by Age, Sex, and Marital Status, Seasonally Adjusted*, table A-10, www.bls.gov/web/empsit/cpseea10.htm.

[2] Bureau of Labor Statistics, CPS, table A-10.

[3] Heidi Shierholz, Natalie Sabadish, and Nicholas Finio (2013), *The Class of 2013: Young Graduates Still Face Dim Job Prospects,* Economic Policy Institute briefing paper no. 360 (Washington: EPI, April).

[4] U.S. Department of Labor (1994), *Commission on the Future of Worker–Management Relations*. See www.dol.gov/_sec/media/ reports/dunlop/section5.htm.

[5] KnowledgePanel is a large-scale online panel based on a representative random sample of the U.S. population. GfK supplies a free computer and Internet service to participating households that lack Internet access. See www.gfk.com/us/Solutions/ consumer-panels/Pages/GfK-KnowledgePanel.aspx.

[6] In this analysis, postsecondary degree includes an associate's, bachelor's, master's, professional, or doctorate degree.

[7] All respondents were asked this question. The analysis includes enrolled respondents who have a postsecondary degree, non-enrolled respondents with a postsecondary degree, and non-enrolled respondents with some college but no degree.

[8] Bureau of Labor Statistics (2014), Labor Force Statistics from the Current Population Survey. See http://data.bls.gov/ timeseries/LNS14000000.

[9] Bureau of Labor Statistics, CPS, table A-10.

[10] Bureau of Labor Statistics, CPS, table A-10.

[11] Shierholz, Sabadish, and Finio, *The Class of 2013: Young Graduates Still Face Dim Job Prospects*. Data for the Survey of Young Workers were collected in December 2013. Bureau of Labor Statistics data in this report were selected for the same period.

[12] Stephanie Aaronson, Tomaz Cajner, Bruce Fallick, Felix GalbisReig, Christopher L. Smith, and William Wascher (2014), "Labor Force Participation: Recent Developments and Future Prospects," Finance and Economics Discussion Series 2014-64 (Washington: Board of Governors of the Federal Reserve System, September), www.federalreserve.gov /pubs/feds/2014/ 201464/201464pap.pdf.

[13] U.S. Department of Labor, *Commission on the Future of Worker–Management Relations*.

[14] Anthony Carnevale, Tamara Jayasundera, and Ban Cheah (2012), *The College Advantage: Weathering the Economic Storm* (Washington, D.C.: Georgetown University, Georgetown Public Policy Institute, August), https://georgetown.app.box.com/s/ vzqem30apzdt4e3vmo9n. In this analysis, postsecondary degree includes an associate's, bachelor's, master's, professional, or doctorate degree.

[15] Carnevale and others, *The College Advantage*.

[16] Paul Taylor, Kim Parker, Richard Fry, D'Vera Cohn, Wendy Wang, Gabriel Velasco, and Daniel Dockterman (2011), *Is College Worth It?* Pew Research Center, www.pewsocialtrends .org/files/2011/05/higher-ed-report.pdf.

[17] Taylor and others, *Is College Worth It?*

[18] Anthony P. Carnevale, Stephen J. Rose, and Andrew R. Hanson (2012), *Certificates: Gateway to Gainful Employment and College Degrees* (Washington, D.C.: Georgetown University, Center on Education and the Workforce, June), http://cew.georgetown .edu/certificates.

[19] Shierholz and others, *The Class of 2013: Young Graduates Still Face Dim Job Prospects.*

[20] C. Stone, C. Van Horn, and C. Zukin (2012), *Chasing the American Dream: Recent College Graduates and the Great Recession* (New Brunswick, N.J.: John J. Heldrich Center for Workforce Development, Rutgers, The State University of New Jersey, May).

[21] All respondents were asked this question. The analysis includes enrolled respondents who have a postsecondary degree, non-enrolled respondents with a postsecondary degree, and non-enrolled respondents with some college but no degree.

[22] U.S. Department of Education, National Center for Education Statistics (NCES) (2013), *2011-12 National Postsecondary Student Aid Study*, http://nces.ed.gov/pubs2013/2013165.pdf. Computation by NCES PowerStats on March 11, 2014.

[23] Bureau of Labor Statistics, Labor Force Statistics from the Current Population Survey, table A-16, www.bls.gov/web/empsit/ cpseea16.htm.

[24] Andrew Sum, Ishwar Khatiwada, Mykhaylo Trubskyy, and Martha Ross with Walter McHugh and Sheila Palma (2014), *The Plummeting Labor Market Fortunes of Teens and Young Adults* (Washington: The Brookings Institution, March), www .brookings.edu /~/media/research/files/reports/2014/03/14%20youth%20workforce/youth_workforce_ report_final.pdf.

[25] Richard Fry and Kim Parker (2012), *Record Shares of Young Adults Have Finished Both High School and College,* Pew Research Center, www.pewsocialtrends.org/2012/11/05/record-shares-of-young-adults-have-finished-both-high-school-and-college/.

[26] Stone and others, *Chasing the American Dream.*

[27] Philip Oreopoulos, Till Von Wachter, and Andrew Heisz (2006), "The Short- and Long-Term Career Effects of Graduating in a Recession: Hysteresis and Heterogeneity in the Market for College Graduates," National Bureau of Economic Research Working Paper 12159 (Cambridge, Mass.: NBER, April), www.nber .org/papers/w12159.pdf.

[28] C. Van Horn, C. Zukin, M. Szeltner, and C. Stone (2012), *Left Out. Forgotten? Recent High School Graduates and the Great Recession* (New Brunswick, N.J.: John J. Heldrich Center for Workforce Development, Rutgers, The State University of New Jersey, June).

[29] J. Godofsky, C. Zukin, and C. Van Horn (2011), *Unfulfilled Expectations: Recent College Graduates Struggle in a Troubled Economy* (New Brunswick, N.J.: John J. Heldrich Center for Workforce Development, Rutgers, The State University of New Jersey, May).

[30] The average number of hours is based on the number of hours worked the previous week. The average number of hours includes individuals who have more than one job.

[31] The Bureau of Labor Statistics defines underemployment as total unemployed, plus all marginally attached workers, plus total employed part time for economic reasons, as a percent of the civilian labor force plus all marginally attached workers.

[32] Godofsky and others, *Unfulfilled Expectations.*

[33] Bureau of Labor Statistics, National Longitudinal Study of Youth 1997, 2013. See www.bls.gov/nls/nlsy97.htm.

[34] Respondents used "temporary" and "permanent" to include a wide range of job arrangements. For example, 72 percent of respondents with a paid job believe that they can continue at their main job as long as they wish. This number includes 14 percent of respondents who described their job as temporary.

[35] H. Shierholz and K. A. Edwards (2011), *The Class of 2011: Young Workers Face a Dire Labor Market without a Safety Net.* Economic Policy Institute briefing paper no. 306 (Washington, D.C.: EPI, April).

[36] Richard Vedder, Christopher Denhart, and Jonathan Robe (2013), *Why Are Recent College Graduates Underemployed? University Enrollments and Labor Market Realities,* The Center for College Affordability and Productivity report (Washington: CCAP, January), http://centerforcollegeaffordability.org/research/studies/underemployment-of-college-graduates.

[37] Vedder and others, *Why Are Recent College Graduates Underemployed?*

[38] Unemployment rate calculated as the percentage of the labor force who is unemployed. The labor force is defined in the Survey of Young Workers as (1) respondents with a paid job, (2) respondents who are seeking paid job, and (3) respondents who own a business or run a nonprofit. Unemployment is defined in the Survey of Young Workers as (1) respondents who are seeking paid job and (2) respondents who do not own a business or run a nonprofit.

[39] Bureau of Labor Statistics, Labor Force Statistics from the Current Population Survey, table 3, "Employment status of the civilian noninstitutional population by age, sex, and race," http://www.bls.gov/cps/cpsaat03.htm.

[40] Shierholz and others, *The Class of 2013: Young Graduates Still Face Dim Job Prospects.*

[41] H. Shierholz, N. Sabadish, and H. Wething (2012), *The Class of 2012: Labor Market for Young Graduates Remains Grim,* Economic Policy Institute briefing paper no. 340 (Washington: EPI, May).

[42] Stone and others, *Chasing the American Dream.*

[43] Stone and others, *Chasing the American Dream.*

[44] Stone and others, *Chasing the American Dream.*

[45] Fry and Parker, *Record Shares of Young Adults Have Finished Both High School and College.*

[46] Gallup Polls, 2014. See www.gallup.com/poll/168704/americansquality-jobs-outlook-improves-april.aspx.

[47] Fry and Parker, *Record Shares of Young Adults Have Finished Both High School and College.*

[48] Fry and Parker, *Record Shares of Young Adults Have Finished Both High School and College.*

[49] Carnevale and others, *The College Advantage*; Anthony P. Carnevale, Andrew R. Hanson, and Artem Gulish (2013), *Failure to Launch: Structural Shift and the New Lost Generation* (Washington: Georgetown University, Georgetown Public Policy Institute, September), https://georgetown.app.box.com/s/ 8tchnjo0wq9meamwwn5f.

[50] Carnevale and others, *Failure to Launch.*

[51] Carnevale and others, *Failure to Launch.*

[52] David S. Yeager, Jon A. Krosnick, LinChiat Chang, Harold S. Javitz, Matthew S. Levendusky, Alberto Simpser, and Rui Wang (2011), "Comparing the Accuracy of RDD Telephone Surveys and Internet Surveys Conducted with Probability and Non-Probability Samples," *Public Opinion Quarterly,* vol. 75(4), pp. 709–47.

In: Young Workers in the Shadow ...
Editor: Nichole Caldwell
ISBN: 978-1-63482-184-1

Chapter 2

YOUTH AND THE LABOR FORCE: BACKGROUND AND TRENDS*

Adrienne L. Fernandes-Alcantara

SUMMARY

Congress has indicated a strong interest in ensuring that today's young people—those ages 16 through 24—attain the education and employment experience necessary to make the transition to adulthood as skilled workers and taxpayers. In the wake of the December 2007-June 2009 recession, questions remain about the employment prospects of youth today and the possible effects on their future earnings and participation in the labor market.

- Over the past decade, teens and young adults have experienced a precipitous decline in employment and a corresponding increase in unemployment. In 2000, their employment to population (E/P) ratio was about 60%. Their E/P ratio steadily eroded even when the economy grew in the mid-2000s. The December 2007-June 2009 recession resulted in record low employment (based on the E/P ratio) for this population. Since the official end of the recession, younger workers have continued to fare poorly in the labor market. In 2012, youth ages 16 through 24 had an E/P ratio of 46.0% and a rate of

* This is an edited, reformatted and augmented version of a Congressional Research Service publication R42519, prepared for Members and Committees of Congress, dated July 11, 2013.

unemployment at 16.2%. This is compared to an E/P ratio of 75.7% and an unemployment rate of 7.0% for workers of prime working age, 25 through 54.

- Recent declining E/P ratios for young people are likely due to decreasing demand for labor generally and youth foregoing work for higher education. Youth may decide to pursue education because of dismal employment prospects and the growing need for more education to be successful in the labor market.
- Throughout the post-World War II period, the E/P ratio has been highest for white youth, followed by Hispanic youth. Black and Asian youth have been the least likely to be employed. For black youth, this is likely due to lower educational attainment. Lower rates of employment for Asian youth are likely attributable to their increasing participation in postsecondary education. Young black males in particular have had the lowest E/P ratios.
- Beginning in the 1970s, the E/P ratios for women increased as they entered the workforce in greater numbers. The gender difference in the E/P ratio for teens and young adults began to narrow in the 1990s, likely due to greater high school and college attainment among females and other factors.
- Lower E/P ratios—and simultaneous increases in unemployment—for young people appear to be due to a confluence of factors. Youth have less education and experience relative to older workers. In general, firms are more likely to hire workers with more experience and availability, which puts young workers at a disadvantage. Young workers may especially face challenges in landing a job during tough economic times.

The consequences of decreasing E/P ratios and increasing unemployment among youth have not been fully explored. Preliminary research in this area has hypothesized that reductions in human capital, such as deterioration of skills and foregone work experience, may have lasting impacts on employability and wages of youth. Some studies show that on average, early youth unemployment has negative effects on incomes but not as strong effects on future unemployment; however, youth entering the labor market during severe downturns in the economy appear to have relatively lower wages in the longer term.

INTRODUCTION

This report provides current and historical employment and unemployment information about young people ages 16 through 24. It begins with a brief background on the December 2007-June 2009 recession and its lasting effects on youth currently in the labor force. It then discusses employment and education pathways that young people today can pursue. Following this section is a description of the labor market data used in the report, which includes labor force participation rate, employment-to-population (E/P) ratio, and the unemployment rate.[1] The report goes on to discuss these data for the post-World War II period, with a focus on trends since 2000. This discussion compares rates based on age, gender, race/ethnicity, and income, where applicable. The report concludes by exploring the factors that influence the extent to which youth participate in the labor force and their prospects for employment. This last section also discusses the possible consequences of decreasing employment and increasing unemployment among youth. The *Appendix* includes supplemental tables and figures on the youth employment situation. The findings of the report are discussed in the summary.

Given the challenges that young people experience in the labor market, this report may be of interest to Congress in the context of workforce development, education, unemployment insurance, youth policy, or macroeconomic policy; however, the report does not discuss specific programs or policy implications.[2]

BACKGROUND

Although the recession that began in December 2007 officially ended 18 months later, in June 2009, many workers were still struggling to find work, and continue to do so today. Unemployment since the recession has been as high as 9%. The recession exacerbated challenges that workers have faced in securing and retaining employment over the past decade, when the U.S. economy had the slowest job growth since 1940.[3] Coined "The Lost Decade" by some economists, 2000 through 2010 saw no net gains in jobs.[4] Against this backdrop, young people ages 16 through 24 have experienced the steepest decreases in employment.

Declines in the share of young people working and labor force participation may be due, in part, to overall weak demand for workers and growing enrollment in high school and postsecondary education. As discussed throughout this report, education is a protective factor for young workers: greater educational attainment is associated with higher wages and lower unemployment.

Nonetheless, recent college graduates face dismal employment prospects in the wake of the 2007- 2009 recession. Calling youth coming of age today "Generation Limbo" or "The Lost Generation," media reports chronicle recent college graduates who are unable to start their careers and instead are relying on their parents or public benefits to get by.[5] Just over one quarter of recent college graduates (from the classes of 2006 through 2011) with jobs report that they are working below their education level, and about 43% of those said their jobs do not require a college degree. Further, 6 out of 10 recent college graduates believe that their generation will do less well than their parents' generation.[6]

EDUCATION AND EMPLOYMENT PATHWAYS FOR YOUNG PEOPLE

For the purposes of this report, *youth* refers to young people ages 16 through 24. Individuals as young as 16 are included because the Department of Labor's Bureau of Labor Statistics (BLS), which maintains official records of employment and unemployment, counts workers beginning at this age.[7] Although traditional definitions of youth have considered adolescence to be a period ending at age 18, cultural and economic shifts have protracted the time for youth to transition to adulthood. Older youth, up to age 24, are included because they are often still in school and/or living with their parents.[8] The current move from adolescence to adulthood has become longer and more complex, and policymakers and others are recognizing that adolescence is no longer a finite period that ends at the age of majority.[9]

Young people ages 16 through 24 may pursue a variety of education and employment pathways. Those of high school age may attend high school and/or work. Youth with a high school diploma can attend a two- or four-year college, enlist in the armed services, or secure part-time or full-time employment. Youth sometimes work and attend school simultaneously. Young people who drop out of high school can do some of these same things, but their opportunities are more limited. They cannot enroll in a four-year college or, in most cases, enlist in the military. They may also face challenges securing employment.[10]

Even young people who are attending high school or an institution of higher education (or those on a break from school) may still want to work, or feel that they have to work, for a variety of reasons—to have spending cash, contribute to their household income, gain work experience, and save for the future, among other possibilities. In a nationally representative survey in 2005, nearly 7 out of 10 high school seniors reported that they expect work to be a central part of their lives, and almost 90% said they value a job that offers a reasonably predictable future.[11] About 80% reported that they valued a job that is intrinsically rewarding because it is interesting to do, uses one's skills and abilities, and allows one to learn new things, among other factors. Nearly the same percentage of seniors valued work because of its extrinsic rewards, including that a job has high status and prestige that most people look up to and respect; allows for advancement and promotion; and provides one with a chance to earn a good deal of money.

Young people can more readily secure employment, especially employment that pays well, if they have some postsecondary education. As the level of education rises, the unemployment rate decreases and median weekly earnings increase for those who work. Among labor force participants without a high school diploma in 2012 the unemployment rate was 12.4%; this compares to an unemployment rate of 8.3% and 4.5% for those with a high school degree or a bachelor's degree, respectively (see *Figure 7* for further detail).[12] The Bureau of Labor Statistics (BLS) predicts that the fastest growing occupations between 2010 and 2020 will require some postsecondary education.[13] Further, in all career clusters, a bachelor's degree or better offers accessibility to most high-paying jobs.[14] As discussed later in the report, the growing need for education to secure employment is likely a major reason why some young people are foregoing work for school. Still, BLS predicts that the occupations with the largest numeric increases will not require workers to have postsecondary education. A high school diploma or less is sufficient to enter 23 of 30 such occupations.

OVERVIEW OF DATA

This report uses BLS employment and unemployment data that are based on a household survey conducted by the Census Bureau.[15] This survey, known as the Current Population Survey (CPS), collects labor force and other data from a nationally representative sample of 60,000 households. The survey includes households with civilian non-institutionalized individuals and excludes individuals residing in correctional facilities, residential nursing and mental health facilities, college dorms, military facilities, and other institutions. Employed and unemployed youth (beginning at age 16) and adults (no upper age limit) are counted by BLS as part of the *labor force.* The *labor force participation rate* is the percentage of individuals in the population who are employed and who are unemployed. People who are neither employed nor unemployed are not in the labor force.

BLS considers individuals to be *employed* if they work at all for pay or profit during the week that they are surveyed.[16] This includes all part-time and temporary work, as well as regular full-time, year-round employment. It does not include unpaid internships. Individuals are still counted as employed if they have a job at which they did not work during the survey week, even if they were not paid, because they were on vacation, experiencing child care problems, on maternity or paternity leave, or some other reason. The *employment to population (E/P) ratio*, is the proportion of individuals in the general U.S. population who are employed. Individuals are considered *unemployed* if they are in the labor force and are jobless, looking for jobs, and available for work. Job search activities include sending out resumes or filling out applications, among other activities. The *unemployment rate* is the share of individuals in the labor force who are unemployed (note that the denominator for the E/P ratio and the unemployment rate are different).[17]

Labor market participation by youth, as well as adults, is a proxy indicator of interest in working. Generally, increasing labor force participation indicates greater interest in working, while decreasing labor force participation indicates declining or noninterest in working. Changes in labor force participation rates, however, are not perfect indicators of individual or collective interest in working. For example, labor force participation may decline because individuals become discouraged about job prospects and give up looking for work. Individuals may also decide to pursue education instead because of the returns they will receive later when they are employed.

The E/P ratio and the unemployment rate can help to gauge market conditions. A stable and high E/P ratio suggests that the economy is healthy, in that individuals are able to find employment. The unemployment rate is also an indicator of whether individuals are able to be employed in the labor force. This rate should be interpreted with caution: changes in the unemployment rate can mask the extent to which individuals want to work. The unemployment rate may decline when firms are not hiring because individuals become discouraged and drop out of the labor market.

In addition to the official count of unemployment, BLS records the number of people who are not in the labor force. Some individuals out of the labor force indicate that they want a job. Those who want a job are *marginally attached* to the labor force if they searched for work during the past 12 months and were available to take a job but had not looked for work in the past four weeks. Marginally attached workers are considered *discouraged* if they did not look for work for one or more of the following reasons: they thought that no work was available, could not find work, lacked the requisite schooling or training, or faced age or other types of discrimination. Marginally attached workers may also be unable to work for such reasons as school or family responsibilities, ill health, and transportation, as well as other reasons for which nonparticipation could not be determined.

RECENT TRENDS

Both the E/P ratio and the unemployment rate provide a snapshot of how well youth are faring in the labor market. **Table 1** provides these and other relevant labor force data for individuals ages 16 and older and by age groups—youth ages 16 through 19 ("teens"), youth ages 20 through 24 ("young adults"), and other working age groups (through age 69) in 2012. The table shows that for workers generally, the labor force participation rate was 63.7% and the unemployment rate was 8.1%. In addition, 58.6% of individuals in the working population overall were employed. Though not shown in the table, these figures represent improvements from 2011, when the unemployment rate was 8.9% and the employment rate was 58.4%. The labor force participation rate was 64.1% in 2011. The drop in the unemployment rate appears to be due to increased employment that has outpaced growth in the labor force.[18]

Teens had the second lowest rate of labor force participation (34.3%), after the oldest workers; the lowest rate of employment (26.1%); and the highest rate of unemployment (24.0%). While young adults participated at a high rate in the labor force (70.9%), they also experienced a relatively high rate of unemployment (13.3%). Individuals of prime working age (25 through 54) had the highest rates of labor force participation (81.4%) and employment (75.7%) and the lowest rate of unemployment (7.0%). Those ages 55 through 64 had a relatively average level of employment (64.5%) and the lowest rate of unemployment (5.9%) among the featured age groups. The oldest individuals in the table, those ages 65 through 69, had the lowest rate of labor force participation (32.1%), reflecting a high likelihood of retirement (and ability to receive Social Security benefits), and a relatively low unemployment rate (6.7%). *Table 1* also displays the share of individuals not in the labor force who wanted a job. Overall, 7.4% of workers not in the labor force wanted a job compared to about 11.0% of teens and 15.0% of young adults.

Table 1. Labor Force Participation by Selected Age Groups, 2012
Numbers in thousands, not seasonally adjusted

Age Group	Civilian Non-institutionalized Population	Labor Force Participation Rate	E/P Ratio	Unemployment Rate	Percentage Not in the Labor Force Who Want Job
16-24	38,783	54.9%	46.0%	16.2%	12.1%
16-19	16,984	34.3	26.1	24.0	10.5
20-24	21,799	70.9	61.5	13.3	15.0
25-54	124,314	81.4	75.7	7.0	12.2
55-64	38,318	64.5	60.6	5.9	6.3
65-69	13,801	32.1	29.9	6.7	Not available
All	243,284	63.7	58.6	8.1	7.4

Source: Congressional Research Service (CRS), based on published and unpublished data from the U.S. Department of Labor, Bureau of Labor Statistics (BLS), Current Population Survey (CPS).

Note: All workers includes workers age 16 and older. The labor force participation rate is the percentage of individuals in the population who are employed and who are unemployed (those who are not employed and not looking for work are out of the labor force). The E/P ratio represents the percentage of the non-institutionalized population who are employed. The unemployment rate is the percentage of individuals in the labor force who are jobless, looking for jobs, and available for work. The share of persons not in the labor force includes individuals who have looked for work within the past year and those who have not.

Changes Since 2000 and 2012

Table 2 displays the youth labor force participation rates, E/P ratios, and unemployment rates for all youth by gender and race/ethnicity in four recent years: 2000, 2007, 2011, and 2012. These four years are notable because they include a period when the economy was expanding (2000), a period just before the start of the recent recession (2007), and the two most recent full years after the recession ended (2011 and 2012). Labor force trends for youth ages 16 through 24 were bleak even before the onset of the recession. From 2000 to 2007, the youth labor force participation decreased from 65.8% to 59.4%; their

E/P ratio fell from 59.7% to 53.1%; and their unemployment rate increased from 9.3% to 10.5%.

From 2000 to 2012, the youth labor force participation rate decreased by about 16%: 65.8% of youth were in the labor force in 2000, compared to 54.9% in 2012. More youth dropped out of the labor force due likely to downward trends in the economy and the growing importance of education.[19] A greater share of males than females left the labor force over this period. Minority youth—black, Hispanic, and Asian—were less likely than their white counterparts to be in the labor force. Asian youth had the lowest rates of labor force participation in both 2000 and 2012. As discussed later in this report, it appears that their E/P ratios reflect their greater likelihood of pursuing higher education in lieu of work compared with their racial/ethnic counterparts.

Also over the 12-year period, the E/P ratio for 16-to-24 year olds decreased from 59.7% to 46.0%, a decline of about 11 percentage points. While a greater share of males than females were employed in both 2000 and 2012, males experienced greater declines in their E/P ratio. Employment for all racial/ethnic groups decreased by about 10 to 12 percentage points. White and Hispanic youth had the most dramatic decreases, with the white E/P ratio decreasing from 64.5% to 49.1% and the Hispanic E/P ratio decreasing from 57.6% to 43.7%. However, black and Asian youth had the lowest E/P ratios in both years. About 36% of black youth and 34% of Asian youth were employed in 2012, compared to about 46% in 2000; however, as noted below, Asian youth also had the lowest rate of unemployment in 2012.

Further, the unemployment rate for youth nearly doubled over the 2000-2012 period, with an increase from 9.3% to 16.2% (the total unemployment rate for all workers also almost doubled over this period). In both 2000 and 2012, males (17.6% in 2012) were more likely to be unemployed than females (14.7% in 2012). Over one-quarter (26.8%) of black youth were unemployed in 2012. This is compared to a 2012 unemployment rate of 14.2% for white youth, 17.7% for Hispanic youth, and 12.7% for Asian youth.

The *relative* change in the E/P ratio was nearly constant for each racial/ethnic group over time; however, the relative change in the labor force participation rate and unemployment rate varied by race/ethnicity. Black and Asian youth experienced the smallest relative change in unemployment at about 54% and 57%, respectively, whereas the unemployment rate more than doubled for white youth and almost doubled for Hispanic youth.

The table also includes labor force data from 2011, as well as absolute and relative changes from 2011 to 2012. The trend over this one-year period reflected overall improvements in the economy, with the unemployment rate declining for all subgroups. The E/P ratio increased generally, except for Asian youth, whose employment rate dipped from 35.6% to 34.4%. Despite these gains, youth of color continued to have high rates of unemployment. At the same time, there was a slight decrease in labor force participation generally and among some subpopulations (except white, black, and Hispanic youth), due likely to still-improving economic conditions and opportunities to pursue education.

Table A-1 and *Table A-2* in the *Appendix* include labor force participation rates, E/P ratios, and unemployment rates for youth ages 16 to 19 and 20 to 24 in 2000, 2007, 2011, and 2012. From 2000 to 2012, teens saw striking declines in their labor force participation (-34.0%) and E/P ratios (-42.3%) compared to young adults (-8.9% and -14.8%, respectively). While teen unemployment was higher, the *relative* change in unemployment for teens and young adults was about even (83.2% and 84.7%, respectively). The unemployment rate for both groups almost doubled over the 2000 to 2012 period.

Table 2. Labor Force Trends of Youth Ages 16-24 by Gender and Race/Ethnicity: 2000, 2007, 2011, and 2012
Not seasonally adjusted

	2000	*2007*	*2011*	*2012*	*Absolute Change from 2000-2012 (Percentage Points)*	*Relative Change from 2000-2012 (Percentage)*	*Absolute Change from 2011-2012 (Percentage Points)*	*Relative Change from 2011-2012 (Percentage)*
Labor Force Participation Rate								
All	65.8	59.4	55.0	54.9	-10.9	-16.6%	-0.1	-0.2%
Male	68.6	61.5	56.6	56.5	-12.1	-17.6%	-0.1	-0.2%
Female	63.0	57.2	53.3	53.2	-9.8	-15.6%	-0.1	-0.2%
White	69.7	62.0	57.3	57.3	-12.4	-17.8%	0.0	0.0%
Black	56.1	50.2	47.8	48.9	-7.2	-12.8%	1.1	2.3%
Hispanic	64.3	57.9	52.4	53.2	-11.1	-17.3%	0.8	1.5%
Asian	50.5	45.1	41.4	39.4	-11.1	-22.0%	-2.0	-4.8%
E/P Ratio								
All	59.7	53.1	45.5	46.0	-13.7	-22.9%	0.5	1.1%
Male	61.9	54.4	46.0	46.6	-15.3	24.7%	0.6	1.3%
Female	57.4	51.8	44.9	45.4	-12.0	-20.9%	0.5	1.1%
White	64.5	56.3	48.6	49.1	-15.4	-23.9%	0.5	1.0%
Black	45.7	40.5	33.9	35.8	-9.9	-21.7%	1.9	5.6%
Hispanic	57.6	51.7	42.2	43.7	-13.9	-24.1%	1.5	3.6%
Asian	45.9	41.9	35.6	34.4	-11.5	-25.1%	-1.2	-3.4%
Unemployment Rate								

	2000	*2007*	*2011*	*2012*	*Absolute Change from 2000-2012 (Percentage Points)*	*Relative Change from 2000-2012 (Percentage)*	*Absolute Change from 2011-2012 (Percentage Points)*	*Relative Change from 2011-2012 (Percentage)*
All	9.3	10.5	17.3	16.2	6.9	74.2%	-1.1	-6.4%
Male	9.7	11.6	18.7	17.6	7.9	81.4%	-1.1	-5.9%
Female	8.9	9.4	15.7	14.7	5.8	65.2%	-1.0	-6.4%
White	7.4	9.2	15.3	14.2	6.8	91.9%	-1.1	-7.2%
Black	18.5	19.3	29.0	26.8	8.3	44.9%	-2.2	-7.6%
Hispanic	10.4	10.7	19.4	17.7	7.3	70.2%	-1.7	-8.8%
Asian	9.1	7.2	14.0	12.7	3.6	39.6%	-1.3	-9.3%

Source: Congressional Research Service (CRS), based on data from U.S. Department of Labor, Bureau of Labor Statistics, Current Population Survey.

Notes: The labor force participation rate is the percentage of individuals in the population who are employed and unemployed (those who are not employed and not looking for work are out of the labor force). Employment-population ratios represent the percentage of the non-institutionalized population who were employed. The unemployment rate is the percentage of individuals in the labor force who are jobless, looking for jobs, and available for work. Persons of Hispanic origin can be of any race and individuals of any race may be Hispanic.

[a] Absolute change refers to the percentage point change from 2000 to 2011, and is derived by subtracting 2011 data from 2000 data. Relative change refers to the percentage change over the same period, and is derived by subtracting 2011 data from 2000 data and then dividing that number by the 2000 data.

Unemployment and the 2007-2009 Recession

The 18-month recession that spanned December 2007 through June 2009, which some have called the "Great Recession,"[20] disproportionately affected young people. *Figure 1* shows the seasonally adjusted unemployment rates for teens, young adults, and adults of prime working age from the fourth quarter of 2007 through the fourth quarter of 2012. Over this period, unemployment rates for all groups steadily increased for each age cohort, peaking in 2009. Teen unemployment climbed from 16.1% at the end of 2007 to 26.8% at the end of 2009. During these same two years, the unemployment rate for young adults increased significantly, almost doubling from 8.7% in the fourth quarter of 2007 to 15.8% in the fourth quarter of 2009. Notably, the unemployment rate for teens increased over the first three quarters of 2011, and then declined (to 23.6%) in the fourth quarter. It increased again during the first two quarters of 2012, and slid back to 23.6% during the last quarter of that year. The unemployment rates for young adults and workers of prime age declined over the four quarters in 2011, but these rates were higher than they were in 2007 and 2008. Rates for both groups of workers reached a post-recession low of 13.2% and 6.7%, respectively, by the end of 2012.

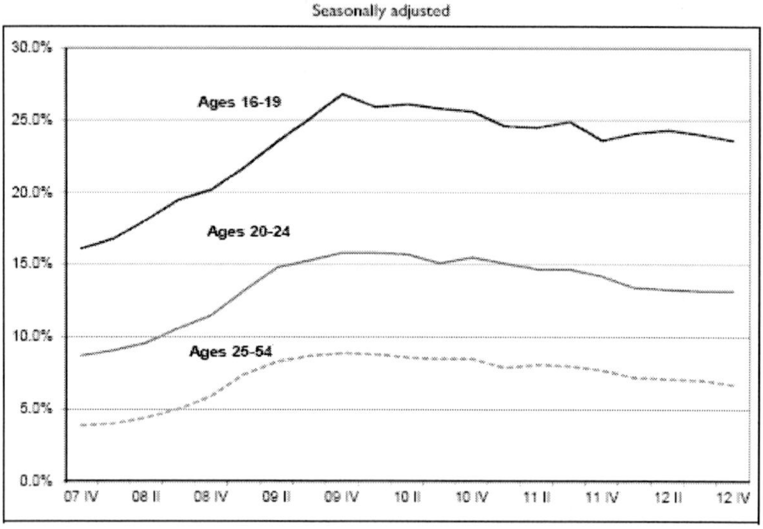

Source: Congressional Research Service (CRS), based on data from U.S. Department of Labor, Bureau of Labor Statistics, Current Population Survey.

Notes: The unemployment rate is the percentage of individuals in the labor force who are jobless, looking for jobs, and available for work.

Figure 1. Quarterly Unemployment Rates by Select Age Groups, Fourth.

Trends over Time

The figures and tables in the remainder of the report include employment and unemployment data over the period following World War II based on age, gender, race/ethnicity, and family income.[21]

Age

The labor market experiences of youth are different based on their age. *Figure 2* shows the E/P ratio from 1948 through 2012 for teens, young adults, and adults ages 25 through 54. (The figure also displays the 11 periods when the country was in recession.[22]) Over that time, teens had the lowest rates of employment, while adults of prime working age had the highest employment rates.

Youth

The E/P ratio for teens was 47.7% in 1948 and reached a post-World War II low of 25.8% in 2011; however, the E/P ratio increased slightly for this population to 26.1% in 2012. In the intervening years, there was variation in the rate—with 42.0% as the average. The data show points at which E/P ratios reached local troughs and peaks. As expected, teen employment generally declined soon after the start of a recession and reached local lows at the end of the recession or a year or two later. Notably, the teen employment rate was below 40% in 18 years over this 64-year period. Seven of those years were between 1958 and 1965 and 11 were between 2002 and 2012. This suggests a fairly recent long-term decline in teen employment.

Also over the post-World War II period, the E/P ratio for young adults was higher and more stable than it was for teens. In both 1948 and 2012, approximately 6 out of 10 young adults were employed. Unlike the teen E/P ratio, which had more cyclical trends, the E/P ratio for young adults steadily improved over the period, particularly following the 1960-1961 recession. This could be due, in part, to women entering the labor market in greater numbers starting in the 1960s. Declines in the E/P ratios for young adults over the entire period were fairly small. The greatest change to the E/P ratio for this population occurred in the last decade, when the rate fluctuated from a high of 72.2% in 2000 to a low of 60.3% in 2010.

The long-term decline in E/P ratios for youth ages 16 to 19 appears to reflect, at least in some part, their withdrawal from the labor market. *Figure A-1* and *Figure A-2* in the *Appendix* show the labor force participation rate, E/P ratio, and unemployment rate for teens and young adults from 1948 through 2012. Over this period, labor force participation for teens was lower than that of young adults. Teen labor force participation trended upward from the 1960s until reaching a peak in 1979 at nearly 58%. Over the next two decades, the rate was uneven. It then declined by about one-third from 2000 to 2012. In contrast to teens, the labor force participation of young adults steadily increased in most years over the post-World War II period. It was stable at about 70% to 80% in most years; however, at the start of the 2000s it began to tick downward, reaching its lowest point (in 2010) since the early 1970s. From 2010 to 2012, the E/P ratio increased slightly for teens, from 25.9% to 26.1%, and for young adults, from 60.3% to 61.5%.

These changes can likely be viewed as partially a consequence of a positive social trend—the increase in school enrollment, particularly for youth ages 16-19.[23] In addition, as discussed later in the report, students are increasingly pursuing unpaid internships to meet high school graduation requirements and improve their prospects for attending college. So although they are gaining employment experience, they are not included in the labor force.

Nonetheless, these trends do not necessarily reflect a tendency toward voluntary withdrawal from the workforce to complete schooling. Indeed, some young people may have dropped out of the labor market because of dismal employment prospects, especially in light of the jobless recovery following the 2001 recession. Although the economy rebounded, the E/P ratios of teens and young adults stabilized or declined in subsequent years. The 2007-2009 recession likely further contributed to the downward trend. The growing unemployment rate since 2008 suggests that some youth have withdrawn from the labor force because of their inability to find work. *Figure A-1* and *Figure A-2* in the *Appendix* show the unemployment rate for teens and young adults. The unemployment rate for teens was between 10% and 20% in most years over the post-World War II period. In 2010, this rate reached a recorded high of 25.9%. Only in six other years—1982, 1983, 1992, 2009, 2011, and 2012—did the teen unemployment rate exceed 20%. Notably, the E/P ratio and unemployment rate for teens converged in 2010 so that about one-quarter of teens in the general population were working and one-quarter of teens in the labor force were unemployed. As of 2012, 26.1% of teens were working and 24.0% were unemployed.

The unemployment trend line for young adults fluctuated over the post-war period, from a low of 4.1% in 1951 to a high of 15.5% in 2010 (and improving to 13.3% in FY2012). The last time unemployment increased above 11% for young adults was during the back-to-back recessions of the early 1980s, when the unemployment rate reached a high of 14.9% (in 1982).

Workers of Prime Age

As shown in *Figure 2*, the employment trend line for prime-age workers 25 through 54 was the highest of the three age groups. Although it was mostly parallel to the employment trend line for 20- through 24-year-olds, older workers increasingly were more likely to be employed over time. From the 1950s through 1970s, workers of prime age had somewhat comparable E/P ratios to young adults, with about 5% more prime-age workers employed in most years on average. Starting in the 1980s, the difference in their E/P ratios began to grow. By the 1990s, about 10% more of the prime-age population was employed than of the young adult population. This difference grew to 14% in 2012.

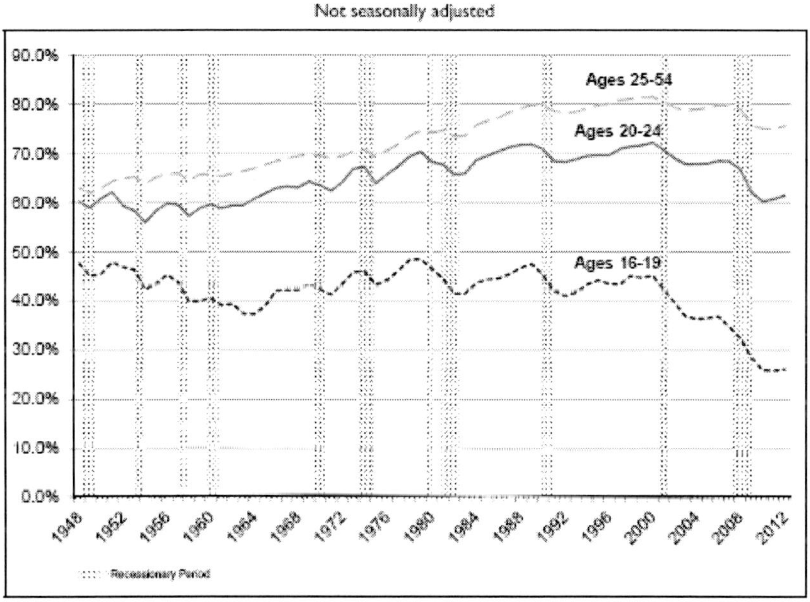

Source: Congressional Research Service (CRS), based on data from U.S. Department of Labor, Bureau of Labor Statistics, Current Population Survey.

Notes: Employment-population ratios represent the percentage of the non-institutionalized population who were employed.

Figure 2. Employment-Population Ratios by Select Age Groups, 1948-2012.

Gender

The employment experiences of teens and young adults have differed based on gender. *Figure 3* shows the E/P ratios for female and male teens and young adults for 1948 through 2012. For many years, the E/P ratios for females were much lower than they were for their male counterparts; however, beginning in the mid-1960s, the E/P ratios for females, particularly young women, turned upward whereas the ratios for males tended to be downward trending. This was due, in part, to increasing numbers of women entering the labor force.[24] At this time, women began completing college at a higher rate than previous generations of women,[25] which has likely influenced the extent to which they pursued and secured employment. In addition, other factors—lower fertility, declines in marriage rates, and increased likelihood of divorce—have played a role in women's increased participation in the labor force, among other factors that are not easy to quantify (i.e., shifts in expectations about gender roles participation).[26] The difference in the E/P ratios for males and females in both age groups began to narrow in the 1990s, but likely for different reasons. For teens, the male E/P ratios started to drop while the female E/P ratios began to rise, so that by 1996 the rates were nearly identical. For young adults, females made significant inroads into the labor market. By the late 1990s, their E/P ratios were virtually the same as those for their male counterparts.

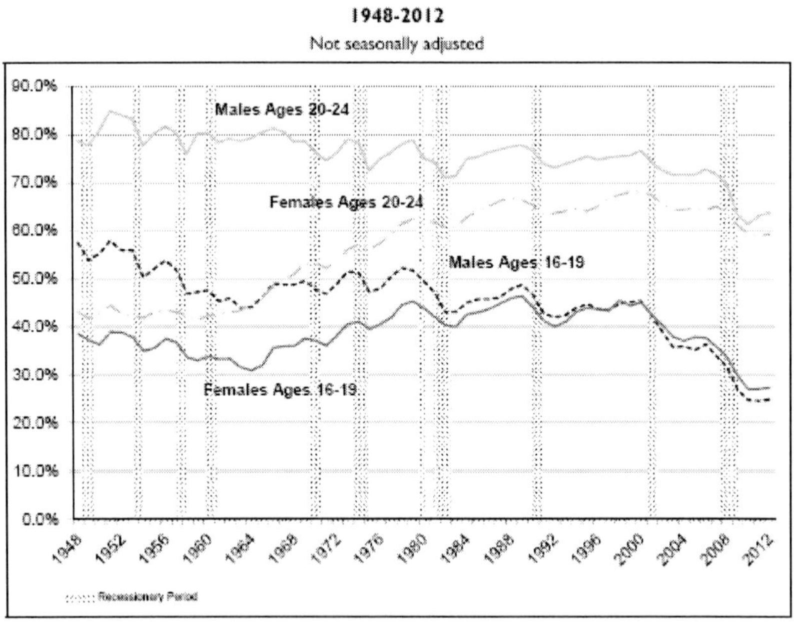

Source: Congressional Research Service (CRS), based on data from U.S. Department of Labor, Bureau of Labor Statistics, Current Population Survey.

Notes: Employment-population ratios represent the percentage of the non-institutionalized population who were employed.

Figure 3. Employment-Population Ratios of Teens and Young Adults by Gender, 1948-2012.

In most years since 2000, the E/P ratios of teen and young adult males and females declined. These declines were greater for male teens, such that the female teen E/P ratio surpassed that of males; however, both groups have experienced decreases in employment in the past few years. About one quarter of teen males were employed and about 27% of teen females were employed in each of 2010, 2011, and 2012. A slightly greater share of young adult males were more likely to be employed: in 2012, 63.8% of males and 59.2% of females were employed.

Similar E/P ratios for males and females may be attributable to the changing employment prospects of less-educated individuals, as discussed further below. Young males ages 16 through 24 are somewhat less likely to be enrolled in high school or college than their female counterparts,[27] and a smaller share of males ages 25 through 29 have obtained a college degree (see *Table 3*).[28] Overall, young males had more negative labor market outcomes than females. As shown previously in *Table 2*, males were more likely to be unemployed over the past decade.

Race and Ethnicity

Youth employment has varied by race and ethnicity. Data on the E/P ratios of white youth have been available since 1954. The data for black, Hispanic, and Asian youth became available in 1972, 1994, and 2000, respectively. In years where data are available for both white youth and other racial and ethnic groups, the E/P ratio was highest for white youth.

Figure 4 shows the E/P ratio of teens ages 16 to 19 by race and ethnicity. The employment trends for white, black, and Hispanic youth (in applicable years for black and Hispanic youth) reflected cyclical effects of the economy over the period depicted, until the late 1990s. Shortly thereafter, the E/P ratios for all groups declined by about 15 to 20 percentage points, with white teens having the steepest decline in employment over the period of recovery following the 2000 recession. *Figure 5* shows the employment trends for young adults by race and ethnicity. Employment for white young adults steadily increased, even during most recessions over the post-World War II period. In 1954, their E/P ratio was 55.9%, and in 2000 it peaked at 75.2%. It then declined steadily, reaching a recent low of 63.5% in 2010, but increased to 64.8% in 2012.

Despite recent improvements for employment among minority youth, youth of color had lower E/P ratios relative to white youth. These lower rates may be due, in part, to the fewer employment prospects of individuals with less education (see discussion below). Overall, African Americans and Hispanics ages 16 through 24 are less likely to have completed high school and college.[29] Schooling may also explain the relatively low E/P ratios for Asian youth, but for a different reason. Asian youth have had the highest rates of school completion for college (and comparable rates for high school completion compared to white youth).[30] The 2012 E/P ratio for Asian teens was at a recorded low of 15.9%. Further, as shown in *Table 2*, Asian youth had the lowest rates of unemployment in recent years, which is likely a reflection of their high rates of school attainment.

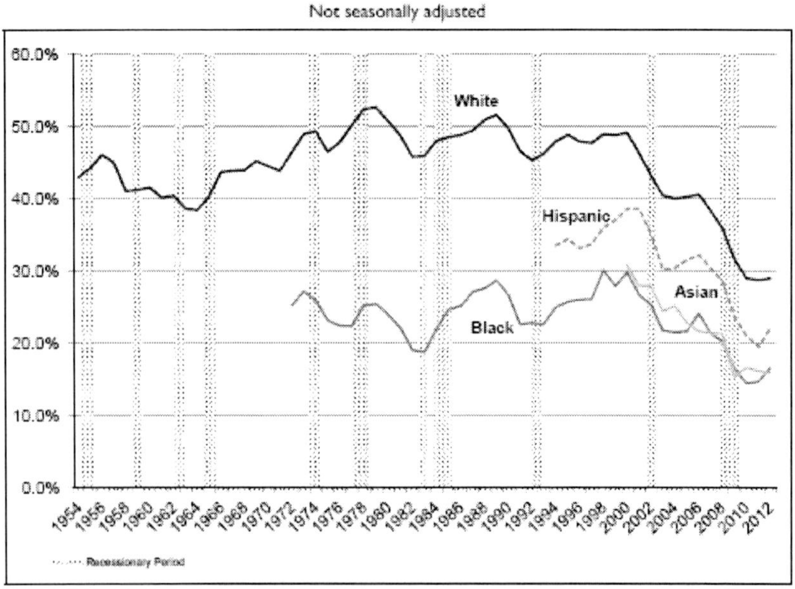

Source: Congressional Research Service (CRS), based on data from U.S. Department of Labor, Bureau of Labor Statistics, Current Population Survey.

Notes: Employment-population ratios represent the percentage of the non-institutionalized population who were employed. The Bureau of Labor Statistics began recording employment data for blacks in 1972, for Hispanics in 1994, and for Asians in 2000. Persons of Hispanic origin can be of any race and individuals of any race may be Hispanic.

Figure 4. Employment-Population Ratio of Teens Ages 16-19 by Race and Ethnicity, 1954-2012.

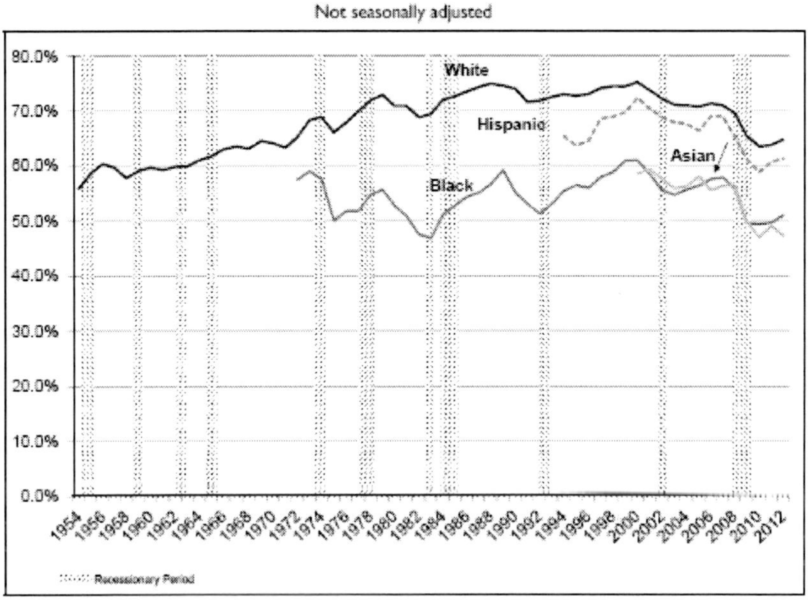

Source: Congressional Research Service (CRS) based on data from U.S. Department of Labor, Bureau of Labor Statistics, Current Population Survey.

Notes: Employment-population ratios represent the percentage of the non-institutionalized population who were employed. The Bureau of Labor Statistics began recording employment data for blacks in 1972, for Hispanics in 1994, and for Asians in 2002. Persons of Hispanic origin can be of any race and individuals of any race may be Hispanic.

Figure 5. Employment-Population Ratio of Young Adults Ages 20-24 by Race and Ethnicity, 1954-2012.

Income

Finally, employment rates tend to vary by family income. An analysis by Northeastern University's Center for Labor Studies shows the summer employment rate of teens ages 16 through 19 increases as household income increases.[31] In the summer of 2012, about one out of every five teens worked from households with pre-tax earnings below $20,000. This is compared to about one-third of teens with household incomes of $40,000 to $60,000 or $60,000 to $75,000, and 37% of teens in households with incomes of $75,000 to $100,000. Further, 16% of black youth with a family income of less than $40,000 were employed in the summer of 2012. Other studies have shown that parents of affluent teens often value work among their teenage children to encourage socialization and to take on adult roles. In addition, families in which both parents work can assist teens to access jobs through their own networks whereas low-income teens tend to have fewer employed parents and may live with only one parent.

The research literature has not explored the extent to which low-income youth pursue employment because of their family's financial situation. While youth may want to work, they may choose not to because of the possibility that their families would lose eligibility for assistance programs. For example, the income of youth under age 18 who are in school is not counted as part of household income under the federal Supplemental Nutrition Assistance Program (SNAP, formerly known as the Food Stamp program).[32] This appears to mean that the income of those youth under age 18 who are not in school and any youth age 18 and older is included as household income.[33] In the Department of Housing and Urban Development's (HUD's) rental assistance programs, annual income is defined as income from all sources from all members of the household; however, this excludes income from children under age 18 and any earnings in excess of $480 for full-time students age 18 and older (unless the student is the head of household or spouse) within the one-year period.[34] Therefore, the income of youth age 18 and older who are part-time students or are working would count. Nonetheless, not all federal assistance programs, such as Head Start[35] and Temporary Assistance for Needy Families (TANF),[36] systematically count youth's income as household income.

FACTORS INFLUENCING THE YOUTH EMPLOYMENT SITUATION

The decrease in the youth E/P ratio is associated with increasing youth unemployment. Both of these indicators demonstrate that the labor market for youth is at historic lows in terms of opportunity. There are many factors that affect labor market outcomes for youth; several factors affect the labor market as a whole and some are more specific to youth. This section provides a brief summary of some of these factors.

The Labor Market

One likely explanation of the dismal employment opportunities for youth is the supply of jobs and demand for workers. In general, firms lay off workers during recessions to respond to reduced demand for their goods and services. In the latest recession, which started in late 2007, the decline in economic activity (as measured by gross domestic product, or GDP) bottomed out in the second half of 2009. Since that time, there is some evidence that GDP adjusted for inflation (real GDP) has increased, albeit unevenly, in each quarter since the third quarter of 2009.[37] The labor market, however, has not fully recovered despite recent economic growth. From 2008, the first full year of the recession, through December 2012, there was a net loss of approximately 3.1 million total jobs. Thus, despite recent growth in the economy, there has not been comparable recovery in the labor market.[38] In general, firms are more likely to hire workers with more experience and availability, which puts young workers at a disadvantage. Young workers may especially face challenges in landing a job during tough economic times.[39]

Experience and Education

Experience and education are also important determinants of the success of youth in the labor market. These factors are not specific to youth, of course, but may have a more pronounced effect on youth because of their relative lack of experience and education compared to other labor market participants. Further, the labor market trends for youth are associated with their relatively frequent job changes, with each transition potentially involving a spell of unemployment. About two-thirds of all job changes occur within the first 10 years of a young person's working life, during which time he or she will work for eight employers on average.[40] This initial period of frequent job turnover has positives and negatives. Frequent job turnover among new labor force members may reflect their trying out different positions and work environments until they find the optimal match; however, it may also reflect employer reluctance to hire inexperienced workers for career ladder positions and young workers in dead-end jobs having little reason to form a lasting attachment to any particular firm. Analyses of data from the National Longitudinal Survey of Youth (NLSY)[41] generally found that while typical young workers do not enter a long-term job (of at least three years duration) immediately after leaving school, they do by about age 22.[42] In a recession, a youth's short and disrupted work history may make hiring him or her less desirable.

Education also plays a role in whether youth seek and are able to find work. Youth may decide not to pursue employment and to attend school instead; they may want to do both, but may not have opportunities to work due to a lack of jobs. The rising rate of school enrollment has likely influenced the downward trend in the E/P ratio for teens and young adults. *Figure 6* shows that the rates of enrollment in higher education among 18- and 19-year-olds and 20- through 24-yearolds has steadily increased over time, reaching all-time (or near all-time) highs in 2012 (the most recent year available). That year, half of all teens ages 18 and 19 were attending colleges, universities, and professional schools—an increase of over 34% since 1970. Nearly 2 out of 5 young adults ages 20 through 24 were enrolled in higher education in 2012, compared to about 1 out of 5 in 1970.

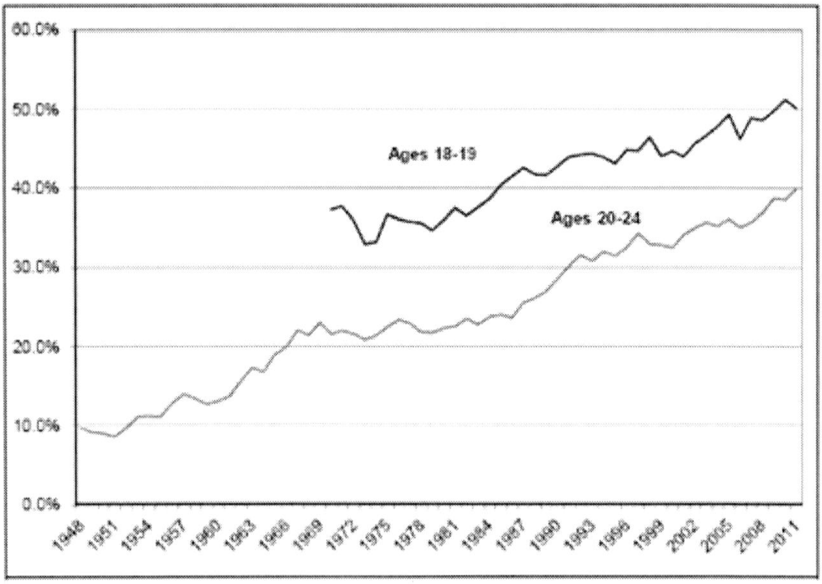

Source: U.S. Department of Education, National Center for Education Statistics (NCES), Digest of Education Statistics: 2009, "Table 7, Percentage of the Population 3 to 34 Years Old Enrolled in School, By Age Group: Selected Years, 1940 Through 2011." Notes: College refers to public and private colleges, universities, and professional schools. The data for 18- and 19-year-olds are not available prior to 1970.

Figure 6. Rate of College Enrollment Among Youth Ages 18-24, 1948-2011.

A Department of Labor study attributes the declining summer teen employment beginning in the early 2000s to education.[43] The study found that the proportion of teens enrolled in school during the summer has steadily increased, from about 15% in 1985 to 53% in 2009. Teens appear to face greater academic demands and pressure, which may influence their education and employment choices. The study noted that more high school students are satisfying the requirements needed for attending a four-year college, and that a growing share of students are taking advanced placement (AP) courses. The average number of credits earned by high school graduates increased from 21.6 in 1982 to 26.7 in 2005. Also over this same period, the proportion of graduates who took an advanced mathematics course increased from 26.3% to 48.8% (the gains are similar for other advanced courses). Teens may feel compelled not to pursue work for the summer and instead opt for volunteer opportunities or internships in order to fulfill their graduation requirements and improve their prospects for getting into a four-year college or university. According to the study, Current Population Survey data from 2009 show that over one-quarter of teens ages 16 through 19 had reported volunteering at some time during the prior year.

Young people may also forego working and pursue education instead because of the gains they can make in the labor market at a later time—although the extent to which this occurs is uncertain. Success in the workforce is related to education, with the payoff being lower unemployment and higher wages as educational attainment increases. *Figure 7* shows the unemployment rate and median weekly earnings for full-time workers age 25 and older in 2012. As the level of education rises, the unemployment rate decreases and median weekly earnings increase. Among adults with less than a high school degree, 12.4% were unemployed and earnings were $471 per week. This is compared to an unemployment rate of 8.3% and $652 in weekly earnings for a high school graduate. Adults with a bachelor's degree or higher had an unemployment rate of 4.5 or lower and median weekly earnings that ranged from $1,066 to $1,624.

Workers with higher levels of education are more likely to weather hard economic times.[44] According to a 2010 analysis, in the past two recessions, "the typical job loser was a high school-educated male in a blue collar job, such as manufacturing or construction, working in the middle of the country. In the past two recoveries, the typical job gainer was a female with a postsecondary education who lived on either coast and worked in a service occupation— particularly healthcare, education, or business services."

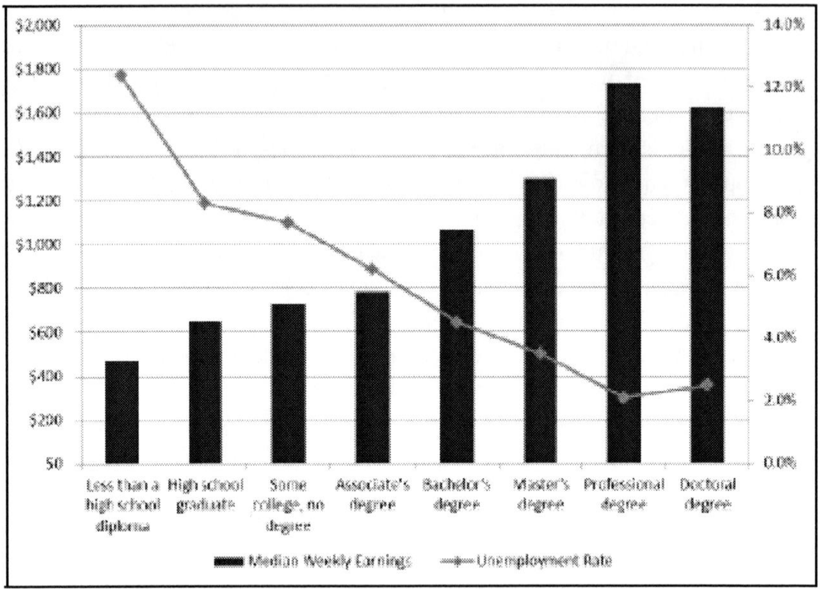

Source: Congressional Research Service (CRS), based on data from U.S. Department of Labor, Bureau of Labor Statistics, Current Population Survey, Education Pays, May 22, 2013.

Figure 7. Median Weekly Earnings and Unemployment Rates by Education Level for Adults Age 25 and Over, 2012.

Certain young people, minority males especially, are less likely to be employed in light of their relatively lower levels of education.[45] *Table 3* shows educational attainment by race and gender for young people ages 25 through 29 in three years: 2000, when the economy was expanding but youth employment was beginning a long-term decline; 2007, immediately before the start of the recent recession; and 2012, the most recent full year for which data are available after the recession. Data are available for all racial and ethnic groups, except Asian youth in 2000.

From 2000 to 2012, females and males made the same gains in high school completion but females were much more likely to have attained a college degree. In 2012, males and females were likely to complete high school at almost the same rate (91.1% for females and 88.4% for males); however, 37% of females had completed at least a bachelor's degree by age 30, compared to almost 30% of the males. In every racial and ethnic category, females were more likely than males to graduate from high school and college in both 2000 and 2012 (except that Asian male youth were slightly more likely to complete high school than Asian female youth, from 2007 to 2012).

All racial and ethnic groups also experienced gains over time, except that the white female high school graduation rate decreased by 1.5 percentage points and the Asian female high school graduation rate decreased by about 3 percentage points. In 2012, Hispanic males were far less likely to finish high school (76.9%) than white males (93.8%) and black males (87.1%); however, 14% more Hispanic males received a high school degree in 2012 than in 2000. A relatively small share of black males and Hispanic males completed college in both 2000 and 2012, compared to white males. Black females made significant gains in college attainment from 2000 (17.0%) to 2012 (26.2%).

Data on Asian youth are available only for 2007 and 2012. A lower share of Asian female youth graduated from high school and a lower share of Asian male youth graduated from college in 2012 than in 2007. Still, Asian young adults were about equally likely as white youth to have completed high school and more likely to have completed college or university. In 2012, about 57% of Asian males and 65% of Asian females were college graduates, compared to about 36% of white males and 44% of white females.

Table 3. Percentage of Young Adults Ages 25-29 Who Completed High School or College, by Gender and Race/Ethnicity: 2000, 2007, and 2012

Educational Attainment		Total	Non-Hispanic White			Black	Hispanic			Asian[a]
by Year	Males	Females	Males	Females	Males	Females	Males	Females	Males	Females
High School										
2000	86.7%	89.4%	92.9 %	95.9%	86.6%	85.3%	59.2%	66.4%	N/A	N/A
2007	84.9	89.1	92.7	94.2	87.0	87.8	60.5	70.7	95.8	98.5
2012	88.4	91.1	93.8	95.3	87.1	89.7	73.3	76.9	96.2	95.3
Absolute Change from 2000-2012	1.7	1.7	0.9	-1.5	0.5	4.4	14.1	10.5	0.4	-3.2
(Percentage Points)[b]										
Relative Change from 2000-2012	2.0	1.9	1.0	-1.6	0.6	5.2	23.8	15.8	0.4	-3.2
(Percent)[b]										
College										

Table 3. (Continued)

Educational Attainment		Total	Non-Hispanic White			Black	Hispanic			Asiana
by Year	Males	Females	Males	Females	Males	Females	Males	Females	Males	Females
2000	27.9%	30.1%	32.3 %	35.8%	18.1%	17.0%	8.3%	11.0%	N/A	N/A
2007	26.3	33.0	31.9	39.2	17.9	19.9	8.6	15.4	59.8	62.0
2012	29.8	37.2	36.0	43.6	18.5	26.2	12.5	17.4	56.8	64.5
Absolute Change from 2000-2012	1.9	7.1	3.7	7.8	0.4	9.2	4.2	6.4	-3.0	2.5
(Percentage Points)[b]										
Relative Change from 2000-2012	6.8%	23.6%	11.5%	21.8%	2.2%	54.1%	50.6%	58.2%	-5.0%	4.0%
(Percent)[b]										

Source: Congressional Research Service (CRS), based on U.S. Department of Commerce, Census Bureau, Annual Social and Economic Supplement to the Current Population Survey, Table A-2, "Percent of People 25 Years and Over Who Have Completed High School or College, by Race, Hispanic Origin and Sex: Selected Years: 1940 to 2012."

Note: N/A means not available. College attainment refers to a bachelor's degree or higher.

[a] The absolute and relative changes for Asian youth are based on 2007 and 2012 data since 2000 data are not available.

[b] Absolute change refers to the percentage point change from 2000 to 2012 and is derived by subtracting 2012 data from 2000 data. Relative change refers to the percentage change over the same period and is derived by subtracting 2012 data from 2000 data and then dividing that number by the 2000 data.

Other Factors

The factors discussed thus far affect the labor market experiences of both youth and adults, although the effects tend to be larger for youth. There are additional factors that have been posited to have particular relevance for youth outcomes in the labor market.

Mobility

Youth tend to have frequent movements in and out of the labor force. The educational calendar exacerbates the probability of unemployment for young labor force (re)entrants. They typically flood the labor market in May and June either searching for summer jobs after the school year has ended or seeking initial jobs upon graduating (or dropping out). While the regularly occurring swell in the labor supply of youth coincides with increased demand for workers in some seasonal industries, this is not the case for most firms in the economy.

Neighborhood Characteristics

Other external factors can affect the labor status of young people. Among these factors are the characteristics of the neighborhoods in which they live, such as area employment and poverty rates, and proximity of those neighborhoods to jobs.

An analysis that utilized data from the National Longitudinal Survey of Youth (NLSY) and U.S. census tract information for 1980 and 1990 estimated that 14- through 22-year-olds who grew up in metropolitan areas with relatively high poverty rates had a lesser likelihood as adults of being employed in the civilian economy or in the Armed Forces and a greater likelihood of not being in the labor force.[46]

Being raised in a poor neighborhood appears to more adversely affect young males, especially those in poor families, than females. Other research similarly shows neighborhood effects can vary according to the characteristics of youth.

For example, another study based on NLSY data estimated that the adverse impact on labor market attachment of young out-of-school males living in disadvantaged metropolitan areas was harsher for those with less than 12 years of schooling.[47]

In addition to social isolation from work due to a dearth of role models and job referral networks, geographic isolation from fast-growing job-rich areas (i.e., spatial mismatch) has been shown to affect youths' employment outcomes.

Some analyses estimated that limited social access has a more adverse impact than access to transportation. Nonetheless, the proximity of jobs was still found to affect their labor market involvement independent of other factors.[48]

CONSEQUENCES OF YOUTH LABOR FORCE PARTICIPATION TRENDS

The consequences of growing youth unemployment and decreasing E/P ratios among youth have not been fully explored in the research literature. The few recent studies that address the effects of youth labor market participation have focused on the individual outcomes for youth and not, for example, on societal or economic outcomes such as reduced gross domestic product (GDP).[49]

The studies found that on average, early youth unemployment has serious negative effects on income but not as strong of effects on future unemployment. Still, other studies show that youth entering the labor force during a downturn in the economy have poorer labor market outcomes in the long run.

Using data from the National Longitudinal Survey of Youth, researchers estimated the long-term effects of youth unemployment on labor market outcomes.[50] They examined the employment status of young men in the sample when they were in their 20s and later in their early 30s. They found that human capital (average level of education and training) increased over time, but also that early unemployment affected both wages and future unemployment. Their economic model projected that a six-month spell of unemployment at age 22 would result in an 8% lower wage rate, on average, one year later.

The effects of this early spell persist; at age 26, wages would be 5% lower than what they would have otherwise been, and wages would be 2% to 3% lower at ages 30 and 31.

Finally, the study found that past unemployment affected future unemployment, but only in the short term.

Studies of the effects of youth unemployment in OECD (Organisation for Economic Co-operation and Development) countries have found similar declines in wages as the result of early unemployment.[51] A study of youth unemployment in the United Kingdom determined that one year of unemployment at age 22 reduced wages by 13% to 21% 20 years later. The study controlled for education, family income, and personal characteristics. Another study found that unemployment immediately upon graduation from college is associated with substantial and permanent future earnings losses; however, the long-lasting effects of unemployment depend on the labor market conditions in which youth are unemployed.

Other research has examined how young workers fare when entering the labor market during a bad economy. One study used NLSY data to determine the effects of white males graduating from college with a bachelor's degree before, during, and after the recessions of the early 1980s (from 1979 through 1989).[52]

The study examined how national and state unemployment influenced the wages, probability of being employed, and occupation type for these young men.

After controlling for the possibility that individuals decide when to graduate from college in light of economic conditions, the study found that an increase in national unemployment by 1 percentage point decreased the wages of the general sample by about 4% in each of the 17 years following their graduation (relative to graduates who left school in 1989, when unemployment was at its lowest point during the 10-year period).

In addition, higher unemployment in the year graduates left school was also associated with lower occupational prestige; however, the effects on the likelihood of being employed and on tenure were insignificant to modest. The analysis of state unemployment rates was more mixed but showed some long-term effects on wage and related labor outcomes.

The study also used Current Population Survey data to examine whether the recession of the early 1990s had similar impacts on workers. The CPS is a cross-sectional data set, and therefore the individuals in each annual survey vary.

The study restricted the sample to white males with at least a bachelor's degree from 1997 through 2006, and found that a 1 percentage point increase in the national unemployment rate when these individuals were age 22 resulted in wage losses for 10 years; however, wage effects disappeared after 10 years. This could be due to measurement error because age 22 served as the proxy year for college graduation (which is unknown in the CPS) when, in fact, graduates may have finished college at a different age.

Similar research used the NLSY and CPS (Outgoing Rotation Group, ORG) to estimate the effects of white and black males graduating from college in a bad economy, except that this study also examined whether employers selected college graduates with the highest aptitude during a recession.[53] The study found that college graduates hired in a recession have, on average, higher abilities (based on the Armed Forces Qualification Test, or AFQT) compared to college graduates who enter the labor market in a good economy.

Both the NLSY (1979 through 1989) and CPS (1979 through 1997) analyses showed, after accounting for a worker's aptitude, that wages declined by about 5% in the first three years of the worker's career. Workers sustained slightly lower wage losses in subsequent years.

CONCLUSION

This report provided an overview of the youth employment situation. It showed that over time, teens and young adults were less likely to be employed than older workers. This is likely the result of their relative lack of work experience, lower levels of education, and frequent movement in and out of the labor force. Perhaps most striking is that the E/P ratio for youth, especially for teens, has eroded over the past decade—even in years when the economy was growing.

The teen E/P ratio has been below 40% since 2002. This suggests a fairly recent long-term decline in teen employment, due to dismal employment prospects and youth withdrawing from the labor force to pursue educational opportunities. While the E/P ratio trend line for 20- to 24-year-olds has been higher and more stable, the employment gains for this population have also been erased. At the start of the decade, the E/P ratio for young adults was about 72%, and by 2012 this rate dropped to 62%. Further, youth unemployment has been at its highest recorded levels recently. More than 3.4 million 16- to 24-year-olds were unemployed in 2012. However, this figure does not reflect all young people who could be working if given the opportunity. Another 1.7 million youth in 2012 were out of the labor force but wanted a job.

The American ethos that future generations can earn more and live more comfortably than their parents may be out of reach for many youth today.[54] Additional research is needed on the effects of recent long-term youth unemployment. Such research could focus on how the current generation of young workers compares in terms of employment and wages to past generations of young workers who entered the labor force during downturns in the economy.

APPENDIX. SUPPLEMENTAL TABLES AND FIGURES

Table A-1. Labor Force Participation of Youth Ages 16-19 by Race and Ethnicity: 2000, 2007, 2011, and 2012 (Not seasonally adjusted)

	2000	*2007*	*2011*	*2012*	*Absolute Change from 2000-2012 (Percentage Points)*	*Relative Change from 2000-2012 (Percentage)*	*Absolute Change from 2011-2012 (Percentage Points)*	*Relative Change from 2011-2012 (Percentage)*
Labor Force Participation Rate								
All	52.0	41.3	34.1	34.3	-17.7	-34.0%	0.2	0.6%
Male	52.8	41.1	33.7	34.0	-18.8	-35.6%	0.3	0.9%
Female	51.2	41.5	34.6	34.6	-16.6	-32.4%	0.0	0.0%
White	55.5	44.4	36.8	36.9	-18.6	-33.5%	0.1	0.3%
Black	39.4	30.3	24.9	26.9	-12.5	-31.7%	2.0	8.0%
Hispanic	46.3	37.1	28.3	30.9	-15.4	-33.3%	2.6	9.2%
Asian	35.8	59.7	21.7	20.1	-15.7	-43.9%	-1.6	-7.4%
E/P Ratio								
All	45.2	34.8	25.8	26.1	-19.1	-42.3%	0.3	1.2%
Male	45.4	33.9	24.6	24.9	-20.5	-45.2%	0.3	1.2%
Female	45.0	35.8	27.1	27.3	-17.7	-39.3%	0.2	0.7%
White	49.1	38.3	28.8	29	-20.1	-40.9%	0.2	0.7%
Black	29.8	21.4	14.7	16.6	-13.2	-44.3%	1.9	12.9%
Hispanic	38.6	30.4	19.5	22.1	-16.5	-42.7%	2.6	13.3%
Asian	30.7	56.4	16.2	15.9	-14.8	-48.2%	-0.3	-1.9%
Unemployment Rate								
All	13.1	15.7	24.4	24	10.9	83.2%	-0.4	-1.6%
Male	14.0	17.6	27.2	27.2	13.2	94.3%	0.0	0.0%
Female	12.1	13.8	21.7	21.1	9.0	74.4%	-0.6	-2.8%
White	11.4	13.9	21.7	21.5	10.1	88.6%	-0.2	-0.9%
Black	24.5	18.1	41.3	38.3	13.8	56.3%	-3.0	-7.3%
Hispanic	16.6	7.8	31.1	28.6	12.0	72.3%	-2.5	-8.0%
Asian	14.2	5.6	25.2	20.8	6.6	46.5%	-4.4	-17.5%

Source: Congressional Research Service (CRS), based on data from U.S. Department of Labor, Bureau of Labor Statistics, Current Population Survey.

Notes: The labor force participation rate is the percentage of individuals in the population who are employed and unemployed (those who are not employed and not looking for work are out of the labor force). Employment-population ratios represent the percentage of the non-institutionalized population who were employed. The unemployment rate is the percentage of individuals in the labor force who are jobless, looking for jobs, and available for work. Persons of Hispanic origin can be of any race and individuals of any race may be Hispanic.

[a] Absolute change refers to the percentage point change from 2000 to 2012 and is derived by subtracting 2012 data from 2000 data. Relative change refers to the percentage change over the same period and is derived by subtracting 2012 data from 2000 data and then dividing that number by the 2000 data.

Table A-2. Labor Force Participation of Youth Ages 20-24 by Race and Ethnicity: 2000, 2007, 2011, and 2012 Not seasonally adjusted

	2000	*2007*	*2011*	*2012*	*Absolute Change from 2000-2012 (Percentage Points)*	*Relative Change from 2000-2012 (Percentage)*	*Absolute Change from 2011-2012 (Percentage Points)*	*Relative Change from 2011-2012 (Percentage)*
Labor Force Participation Rate								
All	77.8	74.4	71.3	70.9	-6.9	-8.9%	-0.4	-0.6%
Male	82.6	78.7	74.7	74.5	-8.1	-9.8%	-0.2	-0.3%
Female	73.1	70	67.8	67.4	-5.7	-7.8%	-0.4	-0.6%
White	79.9	76.4	73.2	73.1	-6.8	-8.5%	-0.1	-0.1%
Black	71.8	68.3	66.5	66.5	-5.3	-7.4%	0.0	0.0%
Hispanic	78.2	74.8	72	71.2	-7.0	-9.0%	-0.8	-1.1%
Asian	63	59.7	55.1	52.8	-10.2	-16.2%	-2.3	-4.2%
E/P Ratio								
All	72.2	68.4	60.8	61.5	-10.7	-14.8%	0.7	1.2%
Male	76.6	71.7	63	63.8	-12.8	-16.7%	0.8	1.3%
Female	67.9	65	58.7	59.2	-8.7	-12.8%	0.5	0.9%
White	75.2	71	63.8	64.8	-10.4	-13.8%	1.0	1.6%
Black	61	57.9	49.7	51.1	-9.9	-16.2%	1.4	2.8%
Hispanic	72.4	69	60.7	61.3	-11.1	-15.3%	0.6	1.0%
Asian	58.6	56.4	49.1	47.3	-11.3	-19.3%	-1.8	-3.7%
Unemployment Rate								
All	7.2	8.2	14.6	13.3	6.1	84.7%	-1.3	-8.9%
Male	7.3	8.9	15.7	14.3	7.0	95.9%	-1.4	-8.9%
Female	7.1	7.3	13.4	12.1	5.0	70.4%	-1.3	-9.7%
White	5.9	7	12.8	11.4	5.5	93.2%	-1.4	-10.9%
Black	15	15.2	25.2	23.1	8.1	54.0%	-2.1	-8.3%
Hispanic	7.5	7.8	15.7	13.8	6.3	84.0%	-1.9	-12.1%
Asian	6.9	5.6	11	10.5	3.6	52.2%	-0.5	-4.5%

Source: Congressional Research Service (CRS), based on data from U.S. Department of Labor, Bureau of Labor Statistics, Current Population Survey.

Notes: The labor force participation rate is the percentage of individuals in the population who are employed and unemployed (those who are not employed and not looking for work are out of the labor force). Employment-population ratios represent the percentage of the non-institutionalized population who were employed. The unemployment rate is the percentage of individuals in the labor force who are jobless, looking for jobs, and available for work.

[a] Absolute change refers to the percentage point change from 2000 to 2012 and is derived by subtracting 2012 data from 2000 data. Relative change refers to the percentage change over the same period and is derived by subtracting 2012 data from 2000 data and then dividing that number by the 2000 data.

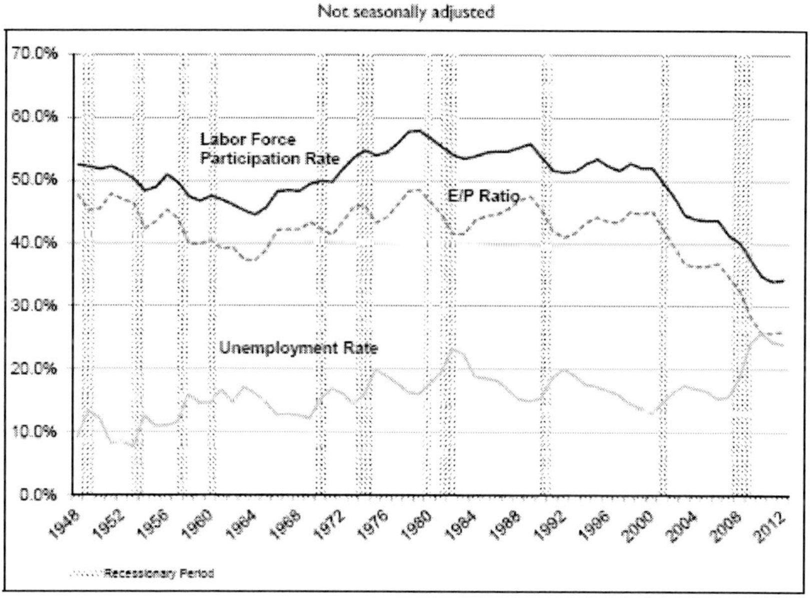

Source: Congressional Research Service (CRS), based on data from U.S. Department of Labor, Bureau of Labor Statistics, Current Population Survey,

Notes: The labor force participation rate is the percentage of individuals in the population who are employed and unemployed (those who are not employed and not looking for work are out of the labor force).

Employment-population ratios represent the percentage of the non-institutionalized population who were employed. The unemployment rate is the percentage of individuals in the labor force who are jobless, looking for jobs, and available for work. Persons of Hispanic origin can be of any race and individuals of any race may be Hispanic.

Figure A-1. Labor Force Trends for Youth Ages 16-19.

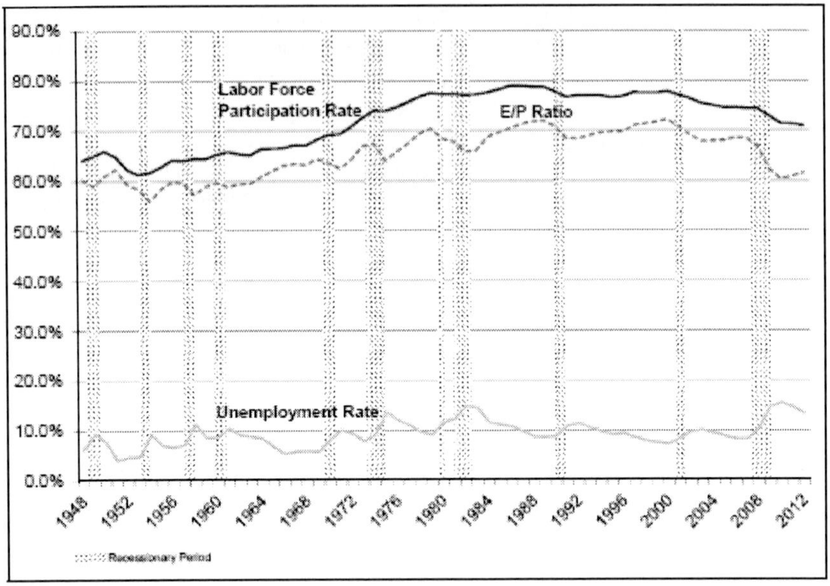

Source: Congressional Research Service (CRS), based on data from U.S. Department of Labor, Bureau of Labor Statistics, Current Population Survey,

Notes: The labor force participation rate is the percentage of individuals in the population who are employed and unemployed (those who are not employed and not looking for work are out of the labor force).

Employment-population ratios represent the percentage of the non-institutionalized population who were employed. The unemployment rate is the percentage of individuals in the labor force who are jobless, looking for jobs, and available for work.

Figure A-2. Labor Force Trends for Youth Ages 20-24.

End Notes

[1] Briefly, the labor force participation rate is the percentage of individuals in the population who are employed and who are unemployed. The employment-to-population (E/P) ratio, is the proportion of individuals in the general U.S. population who are employed. The unemployment rate is the share of individuals in the labor force who are unemployed (note that the denominator for the E/P ratio and the unemployment rate are different).

[2] For further information about programs and policy responses, see Congressional Research Service, Issues Before Congress, Employment and Training Policy and Economic Recovery, Growth, and Jobs, http://crs.gov/Pages/ subissue.aspx?cliid=489&parented =4&Preview=False.

[3] Congressional Research Service (CRS), based on data from U.S. Department of Labor, Bureau of Labor Statistics (BLS), Current Employment Statistics (CES) Survey. The percent change in total nonfarm employment between the first and last year of the 1940s-2000s period by decade is as follows: 1940s, 35.3%; 1950s, 17.9%; 1960s, 29.9%; 1970s, 26.7%; 1980s, 19.3%; 1990s, 17.8%; 2000s, -1.5%.

[4] Neil Irwin, "Aughts were a Lost Decade for U.S. Economy, Workers," Washington Post, January 2, 2010.

[5] Hope Yen, "1 in 2 New College Grads Jobless or Underemployed," The Associated Press, April 24, 2012; Jennifer 8. Lee, "Generation Limbo: Waiting It Out," New York Times, August 31, 2011; and Adam Clark Estes, "More Signs That American Youth are a Lost Generation," The Atlantic Wire, September 22, 2011.

[6] About three quarters of respondents reported having at least one full-time job since graduation, with a median salary of $28,000. Charley Stone, Cliff Zukin, and Carl Van Horn, Chasing the American Dream: Recent College Graduates and the Recent Recession, Rutgers University, John J. Heldrich Center for Workforce Development, May 2012, http://www.heldrich.rutgers.edu/sites/default/files/content/Chasing_American_Dream_Report.pdf.

[7] The Fair Labor Standards Act (FLSA) sets 14 years of age as the minimum age for employment and limits the number of hours worked by minors under the age of 16.

[8] Arguably, the age of youth could be even higher than 24. For example, the Patient Protection and Affordable Care Act (P.L. 111-148) uses the age of 26. Specifically, the law requires health insurance companies to provide coverage to the children of parents who are enrolled in their health care plans up to their 26th birthday. It also provides a new Medicaid pathway, effective January 2014, for children who age out of foster care up to their 26th birthday.

[9] For further information on the transition to adulthood, see CRS Report RL33975, Vulnerable Youth: Background and Policies, by Adrienne L. Fernandes-Alcantara.

[10] For further discussion, see CRS Report R40535, Disconnected Youth: A Look at 16- to 24-Year Olds Who Are Not Working or In School, by Adrienne L. Fernandes-Alcantara and Thomas Gabe. See also Gordon L. Berlin, Frank F. Furstenberg, Jr., and Mary C. Waters, "Introducing the Issue," Future of Children Volume on the Transition to Adulthood, vol. 20, no. 1 (Spring 2010), pp. 1-17.

[11] Laura Wray-Lake et al., "Exploring the Changing Meaning of Work for American High School Seniors From 1976 to 2005," Youth & Society, vol. 43, no. 3, 2011, pp. 1110-1135.

[12] U.S. Department of Labor, Bureau of Labor Statistics, Current Population Survey; Education Pays, May 2013, http://www.bls.gov/emp/ep_chart_001.htm.

[13] C. Brett Lockard and Michael Wolf, "Occupational Employment Projections to 2020," Monthly Labor Review, vol. 135, no. 1 (January 2012), pp. 88, 90, and 103, http://www.bls.gov/opub/mlr/2012/01/art5full.pdf. (Hereinafter, Lacey and Wright, "Occupational Employment Projections to 2018."). See also, Anthony P. Carnevale, Nicole Smith, and Jeff Strohl, Help Wanted: Projections of Jobs and Education Requirements through 2018, Georgetown University, Center on Education and the Workforce, June 2010, http://cew.georgetown.edu/JOBS2018/.

[14] Anthony P. Carnevale et al., Career Cluster: Forecasting Demand for High School Through College Jobs 2008- 2018, November 2011, http://cew.georgetown.edu/clusters/.

[15] The terms used in this report are defined by the U.S. Department of Labor, Bureau of Labor Statistics, "Glossary," http://www.bls.gov/bls/glossary.htm.

[16] BLS also counts workers who are "unpaid family workers," which includes any person who worked without pay for 15 hours or more per week in a family-owned enterprise operated

by someone in their household. Unpaid family workers comprise a relatively small proportion of total employment.

[17] The unemployment rate is the number of unemployed individuals / (employed + unemployed individuals in the labor force) and the employment rate, or employment to population ratio is the number of employed individuals / civilian non-institutionalized population).

[18] For further information, see CRS Report R42063, Economic Growth and the Unemployment Rate, by Craig K. Elwell.

[19] Theresa L. Morisi, "The early 2000s: A Period of Declining Summer Teen Employment Rates," U.S. Department of Labor, Monthly Labor Review, May 2010, p. 32. (Hereinafter Theresa L. Morisi, "The early 2000s: A Period of Declining Summer Teen Employment Rates," May 2010.)

[20] See, for example, Catherine Rampell, "'Great Recession': A Brief Etymology," New York Times (internet edition), March 11, 2009, available at http://economix.blogs.nytimes.com/2009/03/11/great-recession-a-brief-etymology/.

[21] The data are not seasonally adjusted, meaning that they have not been adjusted to account for seasonality in employment and unemployment rates.

[22] These periods are November 1948 (quarter IV) to October 1949 (IV); July 1953 (II) to May 1954 (II); August 1957 (III) to April 1958 (II); April 1960 (II) to February 1961 (I); December 1969 (IV) to November 1970 (IV); November 1973 (IV) to March 1975 (I); January 1980 (I) to July 1980 (III); July 1981 (III) to November 1982 (IV); July 1990 (III) to March 1991 (I); March 2001 (I) to November 2001 (IV); and December 2007 (IV) to June 2009 (II). See National Bureau of Economic Research, "U.S. Business Cycle Expansions and Contractions," http://www.nber.org/ cycles/cyclesmain.html.

[23] U.S. Department of Education, National Center for Education Statistics, Projections of Education Statistics to 2020, Table 21, "Actual and projected numbers for total enrollment in all postsecondary degree-granting institutions, by age group, sex and attendance status: Fall 1995 through Fall 2020," September 2011, http://nces.ed.gov/programs/projections/projections2020/tables/table_21.asp.

[24] From 1948 to 1978, the labor force participation of teen females increased by 11 percentage points from 42.0% to 53.7%. It peaked at 53.9% in 1989 and remained between 49% and 51% until the 2000s, when it began to decline and ultimately reached less than 40% in some subsequent years. Also from 1948 to 1978, the labor force participation of young adult females increased by 23 percentage points from 45.3% to 68.3%. It peaked at 73.2% in 1999 and decreased slightly in subsequent years.

[25] U.S. Department of Commerce, Census Bureau, Annual Social and Economic Supplement to the Current Population Survey, Table A-2, "Percent of People 25 Years and Over Who Have Completed High School or College, by Race, Hispanic Origin and Sex: Selected Years 1940 to 2012," http://www.census.gov/hhes/socdemo/education/data/cps/ historical/. (Hereinafter, Census Bureau, "Percent of People 25 Years and Over Who Have Completed High School or College, by Race, Hispanic Origin and Sex: Selected Years 1940 to 2012.")

[26] Francine D. Blau, "Women's Economic Well-Being, 1970-1995: Indicators and Trends," Focus, vol. 20, no. 1 (Winter 1998-1999), pp. 6-8.

[27] The statistics are available in the following age categories: 16 and 17, 18 and 19, 20 and 21, and 22 to 24. For each of these age categories, females are more likely than males to be enrolled in school, particularly among those ages 18 through 21. U.S. Department of Education, National Center for Education Statistics, Digest of Education Statistics: 2012, Table 6, "Percentage of the Population 3 to 34 Years Old Enrolled In School, by Sex, Race/Ethnicity, and Age: Selected years, 1980 through 2011," June 2012; and Table 221,

"Total Fall Enrollment in Degree-Granting Institutions, by Attendance Status, Sex of Student, and Control of Institution: Selected Years, 1947 through 2011," June 2012, http://nces.ed.gov/programs/digest/2012menu_tables.asp.

[28] U.S. Census Bureau, "Percent of People 25 Years and Over Who Have Completed High School or College, by Race, Hispanic Origin and Sex: Selected Years 1940 to 2012."

[29] Census Bureau, "Percent of People 25 Years and Over Who Have Completed High School or College, by Race, Hispanic Origin and Sex: Selected Years 1940 to 2012." See also, Howard N. Fullerton, Jr., "Labor Force Participation: 75 Years of Change, 1950-98 and 1998-2025," Monthly Labor Review, December 1999, p. 6. In this analysis, which predated collection of data on Asian individuals via the Current Population Survey (CPS), labor force data for Asian youth were combined with individuals who were not identified as white or black. These data were derived by subtracting "black" from the "black and other" group.

[30] Ibid.

[31] Andrew Sum et al., The Dismal State of the Nation's Teen Summer Job Market, 2008-2012, and the Employment Outlook for the Summer of 2013, Center for Labor Market Studies, Northeastern University, April 2013, http://www.massworkforce.com/documents/Summer2013TeenSummerJobMarketPaper.pdf.

[32] 7 USC §2014(d)(7) and 7 CFR 273.9(c)(7).

[33] The program includes income earned in programs funded under Title I of the Workforce Investment Act, except if this income is earned by a dependent under age 18. See 7 USC §2014(l).

[34] 24 C.F.R. §5.609(c)(1) and 24 C.F.R. §5.609(c)(11).

[35] Office of Head Start Program Clarification OHS-PC-I-011, April 23, 2007.

[36] Federal TANF law does not address the income of children, and most states disregard earnings for children (defined mostly as those under age 18 or 19) in school; however, some limit the time that their income does not count. This is based on a CRS review of the Urban Institute's Welfare Rules Database, April 2012, by Gene Falk, Specialist in Social Policy.

[37] See CRS Report R41332, Economic Recovery: Sustaining U.S. Economic Growth in a Post-Crisis Economy, by Craig K. Elwell for a discussion of measuring decline and recovery in the most recent recession.

[38] Congressional Research Service (CRS), based on data from U.S. Department of Labor, Bureau of Labor Statistics, "Employment, Hours, and Earnings from the Current Employment Statistics Survey," http://data.bls.gov/pdq/ querytool.jsp?survey=ce.

[39] Theresa L. Morisi, "The early 2000s: A Period of Declining Summer Teen Employment Rates," May 2010. The research literature is somewhat mixed about the extent to which older workers displace younger workers. Some research shows that older workers are not exiting the labor force but have instead increased their participation, which may make it more difficult for workers with less experience to compete. See for example, Neeta P. Fogg and Paul E. Harrington, "Rising Demand for Older Workers Despite the Economic Recession: Accommodation and Universal Design for the New American Workforce," Public Policy & Aging Report, vol. 21, no. 2 (Winter 2011), pp. 11-13. This analysis concluded that employers substituted older workers for younger workers during the recent recession. It shows that from December 2007 to December 2010, the rise in unemployment among workers 55 and older was countered by their increased entry into the labor market. Further, younger workers ages 16 through 24 had a decline in labor force participation and experienced a greater decrease in their E/P ratio than did older workers. Other analyses show that the employment of older workers does not reduce employment opportunities for younger workers. This research asserts that the "lump of labor" theory—that there is a fixed

amount of labor—is false, and that the labor market is flexible and can adapt to changes in economic conditions. One study shows that higher E/P ratios among older persons "leads to better outcomes for the young in the form of reduced unemployment, increased employment, and a higher wage." Alice H. Munnell and April Yanyuan Wu, "Will Delayed Retirement By the Baby Boomers Lead to Higher Unemployment Among Younger Workers," Center for Retirement Research, Boston College, October 2012, http://crr.bc.edu/working-papers/will-delayed-retirement-by-the-baby-boomers-lead-to-higherunemployment-among-younger-workers/. See also, The Economist, "Keep on Trucking: Why the old should not make way for the young," February 11, 2012, http://www.economist.com/node/21547263/print.

[40] Jonathan R. Veum and Andrea B. Weiss, "Education and the Work Histories of Young Adults," Monthly Labor Review, April 1993, http://www.bls.gov/opub/mlr/ 1993/04/ art2full.pdf.

[41] The NLSY is part of BLS' National Longitudinal Surveys program, which surveys cohorts of workers over time. The primary focus of the survey is on the employment experiences of respondents and other experiences related to employment, including education, training, marital status, fertility, participation in government assistance programs, income, and assets. The research discussed above and elsewhere in this report that references the NLSY is based on the 1979 cohort, who were ages 14-22 when the survey began. A somewhat younger group (ages 12-17) began to be surveyed in 1997.

[42] Julie A. Yates, "The Transition from School to Work: Education and Work Experiences," Monthly Labor Review, February 2005; and Jacob Alex Klerman and Lynn A. Karoly, "Young Men and the Transition to Stable Employment," Monthly Labor Review, August 1994.

[43] Theresa L. Morisi, "The early 2000s: A Period of Declining Summer Teen Employment Rates," May 2010.

[44] Anthony P. Carneval, Nicole Smith, and Jeff Strohl, Jobs Wanted: Projections of Jobs and Education Requirements Through 2018, Georgetown University, Center on Education and the Workforce, June 2010, http://www9.georgetown.edu/grad/gppi/ hpi/cew/pdfs/ FullReport.pdf.

[45] See CRS Report RL32871, Youth: From Classroom to Workplace?, by Linda Levine for a discussion of the role of gender, race/ethnicity, and other individual characteristics on youth labor force participation.

[46] Steven R. Holloway and Stephen Mulherin, "The Effect of Adolescent Neighborhood Poverty on Adult Employment," Journal of Urban Affairs, vol. 26, no. 4 (June 2004).

[47] Bruce A. Weinberg, Patricia B. Reagan, and Jeffrey J. Yankow, "Do Neighborhoods Affect Hours Worked? Evidence from Longitudinal Data," Journal of Labor Economics, vol. 22, no. 4 (2004). (Hereinafter, Weinberg, Reagan, and Yankow, "Do Neighborhoods Affect Hours Worked? Evidence from Longitudinal Data.")

[48] See for example, Weinberg, Reagan, and Yankow, "Do Neighborhoods Affect Hours Worked? Evidence from Longitudinal Data;" Katherine M. O'Regan and John M. Quigley, "Where Youth Live: Economic Effects of Urban Space on Employment Prospects," Urban Studies, vol. 35, no. 7 (1998); and Steven Raphael, "Inter- and Intra-Ethnic Comparisons of the Central City-Suburban Youth Employment Differential," Industrial & Labor Relationship Review, vol. 51, no. 3 (April 1998).

[49] At least one study, from the United Kingdom, has found evidence that spells of unemployment affect wages as well as non-labor market outcomes many years later. These other outcomes include happiness, job satisfaction, wages, and health. The study also found that youth

unemployment involved significant social and economic costs. See David N.F. Bell and David G. Blanchflower, What Should Be Done about Rising Unemployment in the U.K?, Institute for the Study of Labor, Discussion Paper No. 4040, February 2009, http://www.operationspaix.net/sites/politiquessociales.net/ IMG/pdf/dp4040.pdf.

[50] Thomas A. Mroz and Timothy H. Savage, "The Long-Term Effects of Youth Unemployment," Journal of Human Resources, vol. 41, no. 2 (Spring 2006), pp. 259-293.

[51] Stefano Scarpetta, Anne Sonnet, and Thomas Manfredi, Rising Youth Unemployment During the Crisis: How to Prevent Negative Long-Term Consequences on a Generation?, Organisation for Economic Co-operation and Development (OECD), OECD Social, Employment and Migration Papers, No. 106, April 14, 2010, pp. 14-17, http://www.oecd.org/document/49/0,3343,en_21571361_44315115_45008113_1_1_1_1,00.html.

[52] Lisa B. Kahn, The Long-Term Labor Market Consequences of Graduating from College in a Bad Economy, Yale School of Management, August 13, 2009.

[53] Hani Mansour, The Career Effects of Graduating From College in a Bad Economy: The Role of Workers' Ability, University of Colorado, Denver and DIW Berlin, November 2009.

[54] Eugene Steuerle et al., Lost Generations? Wealth Building Among Young Americans, Urban Institute, March 2013, http://www.urban.org/UploadedPDF/412766-Lost-Generations-Wealth-Building-Among-Young-Americans.pdf.

INDEX

D

E

F

G